HOLE IN ONE!

Other Books by Chris Rodell

*Manly Golf: 50 Ways to
Muscle Your Way to Victory*

*When Bad Things
Happen to Good Golfers,*
with Allan Zullo

HOLE IN ONE!

The Complete Book of Fact, Legend, and Lore of Golf's
Luckiest Shot

Chris Rodell

**Andrews McMeel
Publishing**

Kansas City

03 04 05 06 07   VAI   10 9 8 7 6 5 4 3 2 1

Library of Congress Cataloging-in-Publication Data

Rodell, Chris.
    Hole in one! : the complete book of fact, legend, and lore
    of golf's luckiest shot / Chris Rodell.
        p.   cm.
      ISBN 0-7407-3631-0
      1. Holes in one—Miscellanea. 2. Golfers—Anecdotes.
    3. Golf—Humor. I. Title.
    GV967.R73   2003
    796.352'02—dc21

                                            2002044868

Book design and composition by
Kelly & Company, Lee's Summit, Missouri

I've never had a hole in one, hit a megabuck jackpot, or picked a long-shot nag to win at the track. Still, ever since Valerie said she'd marry me—three long, deliberative days after I'd proposed—I've always considered myself the luckiest man on Earth. This book is with love and fond affection dedicated to her. She can't golf worth a lick either.

Contents

Acknowledgments

THIS BOOK WOULD NOT HAVE BEEN POSSIBLE without the exuberant cooperation of the people whose stories follow. Thanks to each of you who took the time to share your happy tales with me. I hope your futures are filled with aces and grandchildren and that each fills your hearts with joy. And for those of you who have an interesting hole-in-one story you'd like to share for, perhaps, future publication, please e-mail me at acereporter @chrisrodell.com.

I'm grateful to Joe Mullins for honing any reportorial and storytelling skills I might have, to Allan Zullo for his generous tutelage. Thanks to Patrick Dobson and the folks at Andrews McMeel for enthusiastically shepherding this project through to completion. Many thanks to my family for the years of golf and laughter that I hope are reflected in the following pages.

These stories stand on the shoulders of all the great work of daily newspaper reporters who decide what ace stories deserve our attention and I especially thank Jack McCallum for his inspirational June 1997 *Sports Illustrated* gem, "Ace Venture." I'm grateful to the editors of *Golf* magazine and *Links* magazine for their assistance and to Evan Rothman at *T&L Golf* for several bull's-eye contributions. Thanks to Geiger & Associates, the La Cantera Resort & Spa, and the 2002 Valero

Texas Open for their hospitality in helping me to obtain many of the interviews with professional golfers. Lastly, thanks to the PGA Tour and the many professional golfers who so graciously shared their thoughts and recollections in this book, the sole exception being Tom Kite, who is hereby invited to go fly his namesake.

Introduction

As a professor of mathematics at Temple University, John A. Paulos earns his living studying numbers, chance, and probability. Part of his work is to make sense of the senseless and to impose an order on seemingly chaotic events. His equations help explain the inexplicable.

What are the odds that someone will get struck by lightning today? How many working stiffs will hit the lottery for multimillions before the clock strikes midnight? What are the chances that something utterly unbelievable will happen today to someone you know?

Or to you?

"The really unusual day would be one where nothing unusual happens," Paulos says. "Given that there are 280 million people in the United States, 280 times a day, a one-in-a-million shot is going to occur."

So what are the odds that someone, somewhere, today is going to hit a golf ball with the unreasonable hope that it is actually going to go where it's aimed and that the ball will travel 150 yards, bounce twice, and roll into the hole? You can count on it. In fact, in the time it will take you to read this introduction, four golfers somewhere in the world will begin celebrating holes in one.

One of them may have hit a heavenly rainbow right at the flag and may be fretting about the inevitable soaking from all the clubhouse drinks he's going to have to buy. Another duffer may have bounced one off a bunker rake and into the cup to win $1 million—some guys have all the luck. Remarkably, it may have been the second one in four holes for the third guy and he feels like he's about to drown from the sudden, unexpected deluge of adrenaline coursing through his veins. Sadly, the fourth may have chosen to golf in solitude, a brief respite from a stressful job and a nagging wife. He just wanted to be alone. And in the clear, cold eyes of golf, if no one else saw it, it did not happen.

Each and every day of the year, 109 golfers on average ace. *Golf Digest,* the hole-in-one clearinghouse from 1952–98, reports there are about 38,000 to 42,000 aces each year—the actual total could be more than double that. It happens to the holy and the hapless, the magnificent and the mundane. It's happened to drunken stooges, pastors, presidents, healthy toddlers, blind grandmothers, and one-armed senior citizens.

Has it happened to you?

The National Hole-In-One Association estimates that an amateur golfer will make an ace once every 12,600 times he or she tees it up on a par 3. Given that there are usually four par 3s on each eighteen-hole course, you'd have to play 3,150 times this year to have a good mathematical chance. Or—who knows?—you might just get lucky your very next time out.

Arnold Palmer remembers his first ace more clearly than he remembers his first kiss. Why?

"The ace meant more to me," the King says with a wink.

What golfer hasn't heard or uttered a small, heartfelt prayer, "Please, Lord, let me get a hole in one before I die." John Meng of Iowa City had been golfing more than thirty years without one when he aced the 160-yard fifth hole at nearby Fox Run on August 14, 2002.

"I'm sixty-six years old and I always said God can't take me until I get a hole in one," Meng said. "When I finally got my ace I went home and told my wife she better make sure the insurance is paid up. She said, 'You finally got a hole in one, didn't you?' For me it was kind of good news/bad news. I was delighted to finally get that elusive ace, but I was sure it was a sign from God that my time was up."

As of now, the great starter in the sky has yet to summon Meng, but his fatalistic attitude is indicative of the hole in one's mystique. Golfers who've led otherwise full, productive lives with happy, well-adjusted families feel cheated if just once they don't get an ace. Those same golfers may have hit multiple par 4 eagles from sidehill lies in the rough—infinitely more difficult shots—but if they've never dunked a 102-yard wedge shot from a manicured tee on a clear, windless day they will go to their graves with it clawing at their souls like an unreplaced divot.

For those golfers who've achieved it, the ball and scorecard are mounted on finely crafted plaques and placed amid pictures of cherished loved ones above the fireplace or in a position of similar prominence. In fact, it's no exaggeration to say that the ace represents the most soothing recollection of all the mantled mementos. Even the best children will do things to make blood pressures and insurance rates skyrocket. They will grow up to date slack-jawed morons, they will sass you in public, they will call at 2 A.M. to inform you, don't worry, I'm fine, but the car's been totaled. The memory of the ace, however, is preserved in sublime perfection, maybe the one moment in a life of toil and disappointment when absolutely everything went right.

Alas, to err is human, to ace divine.

Yet the shot that captures the imagination of golfers and non-golfers alike floats suspended in a relative vacuum. No books exist on the one shot every single golfer dreams of hitting. Golfiana, the Mamaroneck, New York, golf bookstore, is crammed with 15,000 volumes exclusively about the game of golf—none of them are about the ace, something proprietor George Lewis has celebrated three times. The entire aim of golf is devoted to getting the ball in the hole with as few strokes as possible. Shelves and shelves of books at the neighborhood superstore are devoted to the most mundane aspects of chipping, putting, and playing a 2 iron out of high rough into gusty winds. Yet, there are no books about getting the ball into the hole with one swing.

Each and every time Barry Bonds hits a home run, it is dutifully broadcast on *SportsCenter,* and four-baggers are painstakingly detailed on the backs of baseball cards of even the most mediocre journeymen utility infielders. But the hole in one, the only absolutely perfectly executed event in all professional sports, is enveloped in mysticism and awe. Golf, a game that cherishes and reveres its proud history, treats its most remarkable shot like an unwanted stepchild. The 2002 PGA Tour media guide devotes just seventeen slim lines—a silver dollar would cover the entire entry—of its 704-page volume to yearly ace totals since 1970. It doesn't mention player ace totals, ace-friendly holes, or famous aces when each and every fan attending, until the day they die, will say, "Man, I was there in 1997 the day Tiger Woods aced the sixteenth hole at the Phoenix Open. The place went crazy. Nearly 10,000 screaming fans. It's something I'll never forget . . ."

An explanation for the yawning indifference is, well, more yawning indifference.

"There's just not much interest in holes in one," says Dave Lancer, PGA Tour director of information. "Most Tour pros can't even tell you how many they've even had. It just doesn't mean that much to them."

Oh, really? In his book *A Golfer's Life,* Arnold Palmer details the number, date, course, hole, yardage, and club used for each of his seventeen aces. In fact, most pros have had bunches and seem tickled to talk about them.

They all know. Some of them just don't want you to know.

It's as if golf at the professional level thinks the gods on the fairways of Mount Olympus are somehow demeaned when they acknowledge that our most democratically fair game can with a single stroke be mastered by mere mortals. Everyone knows saloon league softball players couldn't throw a perfect game against the 1927 Yankees, but middle-aged golfers less athletically gifted than beer-bellied, pigeon-toed bowlers can achieve perfection with a shot that, at that instant, could not be bested by Hogan, Nicklaus, or Woods on their very best day.

The PGA Tour doesn't care, but the people who buy their products certainly do.

Into the void steps this nimble little volume. It is the first book devoted exclusively to golf's uncommonly common miracle. Its tidy title boasts that it is the "complete" book of fact, legend, and lore of golf's luckiest shot and for an instant or two it may have been. If it receives an enthusiastic readership, it will return with a more complete, fact-packed volume. In truth, no book about the ace will ever be complete because somewhere, once every four minutes, someone is celebrating another hole in one. This book is a humble high five to the man or woman who just struck that shot.

He or she may have slugged it straight and true at the

intended target and watched the ball disappear into the cup with a satisfying click. Or it could have hit some unfortunate bird in flight and dropped into the cup for the inversely fortunate golfer. It could have been struck by Tiger Woods or Scott Hoch, but probably not Fred Couples.

Or it could have been bladed by an elderly blind gentleman whose faded eyes will recover a twinkle at hearing the exuberant news that he'd just achieved a hole in one.

But, guaranteed, about 280 mathematical miracles will happen today.

Some of them will happen on a golf course.

One of them might happen to you.

HOLE IN ONE!

Prose from the Pros, Aces in Their Own Words

THE ODDS OF A competent professional golfer striking a hole in one on a regulation par 3, according to *Golf* magazine, are roughly 2,850 to 1. That means card-carrying PGA Tour players, the best golfers in the world, are quantifiably due to get an ace once every 3,000 or so swings of the club. In the year 2002, the PGA Tour Media Guide lists fifty-one such events. Assuming that a Tour player plays in twenty-five of those sanctioned events, about average, he will have 200 opportunities each year to ace a par 3 if he misses every single cut. If he makes the cut at fifteen of those events, he will earn an additional 120 strokes at the pin on the holes with the daintier yardages. So the average professional golfer—and, rest assured, there is nothing average about a professional golfer—will get 320 opportunities each year to stand on a tee and concentrate his considerable power, expertise, and experience into putting the ball directly into the cup.

And make no mistake: For a professional golfer, the goal each and every time he swings on a par 3 is to put the ball in the hole. They can't survive long being satisfied merely avoiding the big bunker in the front.

The odds say the best players in the world can do what they aim to do once every 3,000 times.

Given their vast experience and the regularity with which they pound balls at a target, it still seems high. Of course odds are statistics determined by number-crunching mathematicians whose right brains are incapable of calculating whimsy, karma, or the indefinable mojo that means some competent professional golfers are blessed with an abundance of hole in ones while others are not.

Why does Scott Hoch, who began his professional career in 1979, have twenty-six aces, while Fred Couples, who began one year later, have maybe a couple? Is Couples doomed by his low-number name? Each has earned in excess of $14 million playing a game that's addicted many into forsaking loves and livelihoods in the vain hope that one day they'll break 100.

Both men are clearly good at what they do; both are lucky to be doing it.

When it comes to golf, good, true statistics are at war with luck, but as any golfer knows, it's better to be lucky than good. When it comes to golf, the odds are just downright odd.

Here, in their own words, are the thoughts and recollections of professional golfers and the times these golf aces have aced.

Corey Pavin

"It's sort of stunning. It really takes everyone by surprise because it's the one time where the ball actually goes where it's aimed. I've had fifteen. There's really nothing like it in all of sports. Everyone out here is a skillful player, but you have to be lucky and some days you are lucky and many, many days you are not. A million things come into play that can mean the difference between a hole in one and just a really nice shot. The wind could gust, the greens could be soft or hard, a spike mark could redirect the ball away from or into the hole. There are times when I'm standing on the tee thinking, 'Man, now would be a really great time to put one in the cup.' I did that and it went in at The Hope in '91. But it's pretty hard to call a hole in one. It is so much more rare than any of the other rarities in sports. It makes a half-court shot in basketball—and that's something that always makes the highlight films—look like a layup. And that's not even counting the fluky ones. That's just the ones that are well struck, bounce twice, and go in. Think about it. Just doing that on a 180-yard hole is a miracle. It's almost impossible to explain. Then you think about the wacky ones that bounce off a tree or off some woman's foot. That's when it gets really weird."

D. A. Weibring

"I've had thirteen of 'em. You should have seen my first one. Really. I wish somebody had. I was playing at the Quincy Country Club while I was in college at Illinois State University. Holed a 4-wood. The thing was I was all by myself. No one around. I stood on that tee for, gee, it must have been ten minutes before somebody came. I didn't think anybody was going to ever come. I just stood there and waited all by myself. Finally someone came up the other way and I yelled for them to go look in the cup. I needed a witness. That was a lonely feeling, just standing there all by myself hoping someone, anyone, would come by and prove I'd had my very first ace."

Joel Edwards

"I remember being upset when I got my first ace, the first of twelve. Just nothing was going right in my game. I was playing really lousy, every part of my game, and then I get an ace. It just kind of reminded me about how impossible the game can be. When I'd been playing good, I never got one. But then when I was playing lousy—boom!—hole in one! It reminded me that anyone, no matter how bad they're playing, can get an ace at any time. Nothing can help you get one when you need one—not even a good golf swing. It's just a truly weird phenomenon."

> *In Ceylon, finding a buffalo with crossed horns and petting it is considered a sure way to bring good luck. Better still, find one and teach it to be your caddie.*

Arnold Palmer

"I remember my first ace more than I remember my first kiss. I guess it meant more to me! The hole in one is always a really big deal. It's very special because it's so unusual. It has a real mystique to it and it always will. I remember one time I was playing at the Tradition with Jack [Nicklaus] and Gary [Player] just a few years back and we started talking about holes in one. Jack tells me he's had seventeen and I said, 'You're kidding because that's the exact same number as I've had.' Then Gary says he can't believe what he's hearing. He'd had seventeen, too. It just seemed amazing. Those totals might have changed, but it struck us all as really peculiar that the three of us—who'd been through so much golf together—there we were, each with seventeen aces apiece."

Jan Stephenson

"My father was always one to say, 'Stop and smell the roses. Savor your victories.' He surprised me after I got an ace when he was caddying for me by doing a complete about-face. He said, 'Now, put this right out of your head. You've got to stop thinking about it. Right now!' He said it could ruin me for the next few holes. I said, 'But you're always saying to celebrate, enjoy, savor.' He said, 'Not a hole in one. It could wreck your round.' Well, he was right. I usually three putt after making an ace. I've had eight and each one means a lot to me. I almost had one last year to win a car at a tournament in Sacramento. It just hung on the lip. So close! I got to the green and everyone standing behind it was pretending to blow it in! An ace, any ace, is a real thrill. And, for the record, my dad never practiced what he preached. Once when he and my mom were playing a course back in Australia, my mom aced the ninth hole. Then dad aced number ten! He went right to pieces, too. He was overcome by his ace."

Fred Funk

"My dad had two in one round. Two! In one round! Man, the only thing I can think of was he must have been really drunk. How else do you explain it? I've had five and every time I made sure I didn't go in the clubhouse so I wouldn't get soaked buying the drinks. My caddie, Mark Long, remembers them better than I do. One was against him and he remembers that best of all because, even with a hole in one, he still beat me. It was on Valentine's Day. After we were done, he took my money and gave me back a ten-dollar bill and said, 'Here, buy your wife some flowers for Valentine's Day and tell her they're from me.' Funny guy."

Brandt Jobe

"It's just a matter of aiming it at that stick and if it goes in, well, you're a lucky man. Lots of people can hit nice shots, but how many of them ever go in? Not too many. The guys who put a lot of spin on the ball usually have a lot of luck getting aces because they're increasing their odds. Think about it: The big spinners get two chances at the hole. Once when it goes past, and once when it spins back. I've had four and I think of my first one every time there's some old James Bond movie on TV. I was in college playing at Bel Air Country Club. We were on the 165-yard fifth hole. I was hitting a 7 iron. We were playing through a group that was waiting on another player. I step up and smack it right in the cup. It's always nice to have an audience, but this was even more special because I heard this famous voice with a thick Scottish accent say, 'Nice shot!' It was the same voice I'd heard say, 'Bond, James Bond,' and 'Pussy Galore.' It was Sean Connery. That was very cool."

David Gossett

"I've only had one, but it was one worth remembering during my most memorable round at one of the most pressure-packed events in all of golf: Tour Qualifying School. I know some guys have said the wheels can kind of come off when they get an ace because it's such a startling thing. Even though we're all aiming to put it in the cup with every shot, it's still such a shock when it actually happens. But at Q-school, that could be fatal. Mine happened on a day when absolutely everything went right. I had had holes in one on a couple of par 3s, but never in competition. When I was standing over the last putt that day, I knew if I made it I'd shoot fifty-nine. I tried my hardest not to think about it. I just did what I'd been doing all day and rolled it right in the middle of the cup for a fifty-nine. What a day. That fifty-nine took me from 129th place down to a tie for 25th. That's a good day's work when you move from 1-over clear down to 12-under par. All that and a hole in one. The rest of the round required some skill, but the ace, man, that's just a matter of taking aim and having fun. It can happen on a round when you shoot 109 or on a round when everything goes right and you post a 59. That's a lot of fun."

Gary Player

"I was playing at the Desert Mountain Golf Course in Arizona with Jack Nicklaus and Arnold Palmer. And we came to the seventh hole, a par 3. It was a double green. The seventh hole and the fifteenth hole shared a green, just like St. Andrews . . . one big green. We came to the seventh tee; the wind was behind us; we stood up on an elevated tee, and I took a 6 iron and knocked the ball right into the cup. Then, I went around the rest of the way and I came back to the same green, this time on the fifteenth hole. And I holed a wedge shot for my third shot. So I had two eagles in the same round on the same green. And Lyle Anderson kindly put a plaque on the back of the green saying, 'Gary Player is the only man to eagle the seventh and the fifteenth in the same round.' So, I'd say that was probably my most significant hole in one. Then, with my wife having had two holes in one in the same round (which she keeps reminding me about), I have since had this on my mind and I wanted to try and achieve this. So, after my two eagles, we came to the seventeenth hole, which is a par 3; I hit the shot and the ball actually went right around the cup and stopped on the edge. I would have given anything to go to my wife and tell her than I had two holes in one as well, but it never worked. And she keeps reminding me that she has beaten me at that every week of my life!"

Bo Van Pelt

"I've had two and hit a lot that came really close, but the one I'll probably never forget as long as I live is the one I saw in high school. A kid on my high school team hit a 3 wood on a 160-yard hole and it rolled on the ground for the last 100 yards or so and wound up right in the hole. I still can't believe it. How do you explain something like that? There's guys that golf all their lives—good golfers—and they never get even one. Then a kid gets one like that after it's taken a couple of dozen bounces along the ground. Strange, strange game."

Kelly Gibson

"I've had seven. The first came after a really big debate with my college coach at Lamar University. I'll never forget it. It was a 219-yard hole over water. He kept insisting I hit a 4 iron and I told him there was no way I could get there with a 4 iron. I needed a 3. We went back and forth and he was getting pretty hot so I told him I'd hit the 4. Well, of course, I wasn't going to do that. I sneaked back and grabbed the 3 iron and ran up to the tee. Wouldn't you know it, I hit the thing right in for a hole in one. Without even congratulating me, he comes running up and starts yelling, 'You hit the 3, didn't you! You hit the 3!' I'm saying, 'See! See! I told you so! I told you the 3 was the right club! See!' That really was one of the all-time I-told-you-so's 'cause how's he going to argue? He starts telling me, 'Now, don't let it ruin your round!

You've still got a lot of golf to play.' Next shot—thud!—a little dribbler right in the drink. Round over. But that doesn't always happen like that. One time at Torrey Pines in San Diego, I aced the eighth hole. The next hole's a par 5. I hit a booming drive and then nail a 3 wood that hit the cup and bounced out. I was playing with Fred Funk and he starts laughing and says, 'Man, there's no way the golf gods are going to give you something like that after a hole in one! No way!' He was right, but I did wind up with three eagles on the scorecard that day."

Mark Brooks

"Maybe I'm crazy, but the hole in one doesn't mean all that much to me. I've had fifteen and to me it's just another shot. After you've made your first four or so, it's really just another number on the scorecard. It's not an indicator that you're a good golfer or not. Heck, back in the summer of '99, I had one a month for five straight months and I was playing some really terrible golf. I couldn't score or do much to make a cut when it counted, but I was sure getting a lot of aces. Big deal."

Notah Begay III

"How do you explain it? It's the strangest shot in golf. I saw one that bounced off a tree and went in the cup. If that tree's not there, the guy's looking at a double bogey. Even with the tree being there, who's to say it's not going to bounce the other way or just fall straight down. That's what you'd expect would happen. But this time it hits the branch just so and bounces on the green and rolls in the cup. I've had five. Don't ask me how. If I knew I'd do it every time. Believe me, that's the secret we're all after. How to get the ball in the hole."

Jeff Gove

"'You missed it. Man, you missed it again.' I had this friend of mine caddie for me one time. He was in a rock band and didn't know anything about golf. I'd hit a really good shot from 170 yards out and put it within eight feet of the hole and be really proud and he'd say, 'Man, what's good about that? You missed.' And you know what? He was right. He didn't know anything about golf, but he knew the object is to put the ball in the hole every single time. I've had five aces, but I still think about that guy whenever I hit a really good shot to about five feet away. Yeah, that's a good shot, but I missed."

Doug Sanders

"I got my first at the seventh hole at a club in Cedartown, Georgia. I was seventeen years old and remember I did it with a Spalding Dot 2. One month to the day later I was standing on the tee of the same hole. I remember reaching into my bag for a cigarette and seeing that same Spalding 2 that I'd used for my first ace. I pulled it out, teed it up, and put it right in the hole. Just like the last time. I don't know what happened to it. I gave it to some girl and told her it was my lucky hole-in-one ball. Never saw it again. I've had seventeen aces in regulation. I've had thirty at corporate outings where you stand there at a tee of a par 3 and fire at the pin with every foursome that comes through. I usually give the greenskeeper some money to put it in a place where I have a good chance of acing. A hole in one is special to amateur golfers because they may never get another one. Pros figure they're going to get bunches. It's like for some girl winning a beauty contest in high school. To her it's a really big deal.

But for someone like Miss Universe, she's already won maybe fifteen or twenty other beauty contests. One more beauty contest is not that big a deal."

Tiger Woods

"I've had eighteen, seven in competition. I had my first professional ace at my first professional tournament, the Greater Milwaukee Open in 1996. That was cool. One time I hit the hole on the fly and it bounced out and went straight into a bunker. It's all a matter of hitting the ball in the right direction. From there, it's all luck."

David Frost

"I don't think of myself as superstitious, but I will never play with a green tee. One time I was using a green tee and a guy I was playing with said, 'Oh, you should never use a green tee! Bad luck! I never use 'em. Never will.' I just kind of laughed, but then I hit right into trouble and never recovered. Just a terrible hole. I threw that green tee away and have never used one since. On the par 3s I try and aggressively play away from the flag. I want to put it as close to the flag as possible without letting the hazards and threats come into play. I've had five, but I don't consider myself a lucky golfer. Everything I've accomplished, I've earned the hard way."

Patty Berg

"I had the first hole in one in the history of the LPGA—and what a thrill! It was the seventh hole at the 1959 Churchill Valley Country Club near Pittsburgh. Didn't get another one in competition ever again. Can you believe that? But I got the first and it was great. I didn't see it go in. It was an uphill par 3. I didn't think I hit it that good, but then all the people around the green started jumping up and down—woooo! I knew it was in. It was the first hole in one ever made in LPGA competition. I was thrilled to death. I had a couple others in regular rounds, but that was my first and last one in competition. I wish I'd have had more, but I got the first. That's what mattered. As soon as it went in, I knew it would be remembered forever."

Bob Estes

"A hole in one is the one time when you don't feel like professional golf is selfish. Score a hole in one and everyone in the gallery feels like you did it for them. And that feels great. I still have people that come up to me and say, 'Hey, I was there when you aced the fourteenth hole at TPC at Southwind. Man, I'll never forget it as long as I live.' That one was really special. I've been going to Memphis for that tournament for fourteen of fifteen years and won there in 2001. I always stay with the same family. I've made a lot of friends there and have a real loyal following. That hole's been a real nemesis for me, too. To ace it in front of all those friends was great. I ran around and did the Hale Irwin at Medinah thing and tried to high five everyone in the gallery. People think it's something they'll never forget? Well, man, neither will I. That was a thrill. I sent the ball and the scorecard to my mom and she's going to have them put on a plaque so I can keep it on my desk. It was real special."

Stan Utley

"Did you know that a regulation golf cup will hold four balls? Try it sometime. You can drop four golf balls straight in. That means there's room enough for some lucky foursome, but I don't think that's ever going to happen. I've had five aces. One of them came at a pro-am on the Nike tour a few years ago outside of Greenville, South Carolina. It was a blind uphill shot. I took a 4 iron and thought I'd hit a pretty good one. I got up there and there were two ladies sitting on chairs beside the green. One of them said real casually, 'One of the balls went in the hole.' I looked and it was mine. They were giving away prizes and I was real excited because I wasn't making a lot of money back then. I was hoping for a car or something. Instead, they told me I'd won two tickets to the U.S. Open. Now, I go to a golf tournament almost every week of my life. That was the last thing I wanted. Then they told me I could cash them out for $6,000. I took it right away. That was a lot of money to me back then."

Ben Crenshaw

"I was thirteen years old and had been golfing for six years when I finally got my first ace. Then two days later I got another one! I thought, man, I must have finally figured it all out and they were going to drop for me all the time. Well, of course, that didn't happen. I have had eighteen. Now if I go two or three years without one I start to wonder if I'll ever get another one. I sure hope so. It's one of the great feelings in all of golf. It's just so unexpected. I had one on number eight at St. Andrews and my father was there watching. For me, it doesn't get any better than that. If you could pick one course in the world to have an ace, that would be it. And to have your father standing there, it was the greatest. We just looked at each other with a look I'll never forget as long as I live. It was so unexpected and it was the only one of mine he's ever seen. What a memory."

Lee Trevino

"I'm the only guy in the world who can't tell you how many tournaments I've won or total aces I've had. I'm just always looking forward. I've had six in competition, and that's counting the two that everyone remembers. The Skins game in '87 and the one for $1 million at Rick Smith's Par 3 Shootout at Treetops Resort in Gaylord, Michigan. For me, it doesn't surprise me when a ball goes in the hole because, man, that's where I'm aiming. People say, 'Boy, you're one lucky son of a gun to get a hole in one.' I tell them I'd be lucky if I was aiming to put it in the big right bunker and then it went in the hole. Now that's lucky. I saw a guy do that in the Philippines once. His shot was heading for a bunker and he got so mad he snapped his club right in two while the ball was still in the air. It's heading straight for that bunker and hits the lip, bounces on the green, and rolls in the hole. The guy's standing there holding his club in two pieces and he'd just had a hole in one. We told him, 'It ain't over till the fat lady sings.' The hole in one is special because it's the only thing in golf that's perfect. The reason more amateurs don't get them is the ball never goes where they aim it. If they aimed somewhere else they'd probably get one once in a while."

Mac O'Grady

"A hole in one is amazing when you think of all the different universes this white mass of molecules has to pass through on its way to the hole."

Beginnings

FOG FROM ST. ANDREWS BAY laces up and down Market, South, and North streets of the old Scottish town that is the revered cradle of the grand old game of golf. Off in the distance, a lone bagpiper keens a mournful blare into the chilly dawn. Yawn-stifling caddies and starry-eyed golf pilgrims begin their march past the Road Hole to queue up before the cramped box with the sign "Old Course Starter" that sits in the shadows of the venerable Royal and Ancient Clubhouse. The golfers speak in hushed tones and admit to uttering secular sorts of prayers that their name will be drawn and a thick Scottish accent will announce that within the hour they will have lived the long-simmering dream of stroking a ball along the rolling fairways of the Old Course at St. Andrews.

Then, from out of the mist appears a bearded old gentleman leaning on an inverted golf club as his steadying cane. Snow-white whiskers fall from his chin clear down to his chest. He speaks and the morning-weary caddies brighten.

"Aye, 'tis a bonny day for golf in the Auld Gray Toon."

Could it be?

It is! Old Tom Morris, golf's original legend, back from the dead after nearly 100 years moldering in the grave.

Talk about your amazing recovery shots.

He's as good a man as any to describe golf's first recorded hole in one. After all, he was there.

"Yes, it was young Tommy at the station hole, what was then number eight, at Prestwick. It was September 22, 1869, the third of his four consecutive Open Championships. He bested me by three strokes that year. Imagine that, a father and son finishing the championships first and second. Take that Earl Woods! I was as proud that day as if I'd won it myself. Ah, young Tommy, aye, a finer golfer there ne'er lived. He'd have won a dozen more if he hadn't died. Taken in his prime, he was, at just twenty-four years old. His dear wife, Margaret, aye, a striking red-haired woman to whom he'd been married for just one year, had died during childbirth. What a bonny couple they made. Tommy passed on Christmas Day just four months later. They said he'd died of a broken heart. Aye, had that been true, then how could I have lived?"

Uh, sir?

"Yes?"

That's a good question. How could you have lived? I mean, you're, what, 181 years old. I mean you're now Really, Really Old Tom Morris.

The jig is up. Old Tom Morris is really an aptly named man called Joy, David Joy. A native St. Andrean, the fifty-three-year-old Joy is a golf author, artist, historian, and actor who's performed the role of Old Tom Morris for legions of delighted golf fans, including Prince Andrew. His studio sits one mile outside of St. Andrews and overlooks the town and the fabled links. The studio where he began earning his living painting golf scenes has grown into a museum for the game and a shrine to Old Tom Morris and the course he called home. Even the garden has a reproduction of the Old Course starter's box—

a converted Victorian Bathing Hut that was wheeled onto the course in 1890. He'd earned acclaim for his depictions of his forefathers swatting at the heather and the scenes that captured the essence of the early days of golf. While waiting for the paint to dry, he immersed himself in auld towne history and soon began performing as Old Tom for the tourists who were eager to learn about the soul-warming game.

"I just kind of grew into the role," says Joy. "My great-grandfather was a registered caddie for Old Tom Morris in 1892 and my grandfather was a club maker with Auchter-lonies, up until the transitional period of hickory to steel shafts. When I started doing Old Tom, I'd carry along a scrapbook of items I'd retrieved from the wonderful archives of the early spring and autumn meetings of the Royal and Ancient. For me the scrapbook was a theater prop, but Prince Andrew attended one of my performances and showed a keen interest in the scrapbook. It gave me the idea to compile it for proper publication."

The book, *The Scrapbook of Old Tom Morris,* (Sleeping Bear Press, 2001), is a treasure trove of authentic history, fact, and gossip straight from the pen of the man who put golf on the map. It pays homage to the son Morris sired who, before he died at the age of twenty-four, had already established himself as one of the greatest golfers ever and the one who hit the first ace ever recorded.

The 145-yard shot was such a remarkable event that the unnamed reporter for the local *Advertiser* could not find the words to concisely describe what he'd witnessed. The clip from September 23, 1869, reads:

"Prestwick Golf Club: The competition for the championship belt of the Prestwick Golf Club came off on the Prestwick Links on Thursday, and was witnessed by a large number of spectators. The weather was very favorable for the game, and great interest was manifested in it . . .

"There was some capital play. After the first round, however, it was almost certain that Tom Morris, jun. would repeat his last year's performance by carrying off the belt—he having made the first round in 50 strokes.

"Curiously enough the station hole was made by him in one stroke."

There it is. The very first ace, like so many that followed, was an X-file. It could not be comprehended. It was and remains a curiosity, an inexplicable event. The writer seems to be saying, "Hey, I just report this stuff. You can believe it or not." You can almost bet that Young Tom Morris walked into the clubhouse and someone called him a blasted liar—then demanded he buy them a drink.

Curiously enough, Jim Scheller got not one, but two aces in one charmed round at the Golden Valley Country Club near Minneapolis and eagerly began phoning friends to share the good news. "I called a couple of guys," Scheller told the Minneapolis-St. Paul area *Star Tribune.* "One of them said I must have been drinking. The other guy hung up on me."

Curiously enough, that's often the reaction to a hole in one, any hole in one. In fact, the most common words heard immediately after the spoken phrase "I just had a hole in one" are "You're kidding me," or some form of incredulity in which bovine excrement is the principle expression of disbelief.

⌣ ●

Young Tom Morris is credited with the first recorded ace, but ol' Tom Jewell, seventy-two, claims to have achieved the earliest ace and there is no evidence to the contrary.

"We had a 6:30 A.M. tee time at Gull Lake View Golf Course in Kalamazoo, Michigan," said the Oldsmar, Florida, grandfather. "The second hole was 145 yards. I hit a 9 iron. Never saw it go in. I bent over to pick up my tee and the ball dropped. It was 6:45 A.M., Memorial Day, 1977. It has to be among the earliest aces ever recorded, if not the earliest."

Jewell is no average golfer. In fact, his credentials stipulate that he be referred to as a golf authority and his word is not to disputed. He was the 1997 Golf Nut of the Year and he has been inducted into the Golf Nuts Society Hall of Fame. The Golf Nuts Society (www.golfnuts.com) was founded in 1986 by head nut Ron Garland and is for people who do things like practice imaginary chip shots with invisible wedges in places like elevators, or for anyone who suffered a golf-related divorce. Garland says he formed the group to prove to himself that he wasn't a crazy person, that he was just crazy about golf.

The reasons Jewell was named Golf Nut of the Year include:

- He played golf on the first day of his honeymoon, April 8, 1956, in thirty-one-degree temperatures with snow on the ground and he convinced his bride, Lavon, to walk all eighteen holes with him. They've been married forty-six years.
- A back injury led his doctor to prescribe three weeks flat on his back in bed. During the second supine week, a friend called with a first-time invitation to play Augusta National. The doctor said he could play if he didn't move for ten days. He wound up emerging from bed in time to play Augusta on his fifty-fifth birthday.
- He's collected more than 5,130 logo balls.
- Each Monday since 1992, he's dutifully sat down and written congratulatory letters to the winners of all PGA,

LPGA, and Senior PGA Tour events, and his devotion to the game has earned him invitations to golf with 130 of the professionals in the past twenty years.

• And he's had three aces, which the Golf Nuts recognize because it has absolutely nothing to do with skill.

In addition, during the first ten months of 2002, he'd already shot or beat his age of seventy-two eight times. So, when Tom Jewell says he's had the earliest ace in history, who's going to dispute him? When it comes to golf authority, this Jewell really sparkles.

Blessed Strokes of Luck

For many, acing a hole is so incomprehensible they offer heavenly intervention for why their good fortune occurred. Any number of deities, sacred and pagan, are cited for the reason why the ball preposterously went where it was supposed to. Men and women who rarely attend church, who, in fact skip church to golf, often think agents of the Almighty had a hand in their earthly good fortune.

Dale Wilbur thinks God wanted him to ace the 165-yard eighth hole at Berry Creek Country Club in Round Rock, Texas, and he makes some good points on His behalf.

"I think He knew how much joy it would bring me and others," Wilbur says. "I'd been playing thirty-two years and I'd never had one. If I finally had an ace on that day, others would see that God was working through me. It's a real mysterious thing. The wind was blowing in my face and I had a 6 iron and thought about it over and over. But instead, I grabbed a 7 and the wind just died. What's the probability of that? That's why I think God wanted me to ace. He knew it would bring great joy unto Him when I did."

Wilbur's a fine, pleasant fellow with a warm grin and a

ready laugh, the sort any golfer would enjoy sharing a cart and eighteen sunny holes with. But there are lots of golfers who fit that description. Why Wilbur? Why did God want Wilbur to ace and not millions of other good-hearted golfers who die an aceless death?

Could it be that he's the music minister of the First Baptist Church in Georgetown, Texas? And that there was a $20,000 Chevy Blazer or cash equivalent available for anyone acing that hole that day and, gee, the church could really use the money? Could it be that simple? When it comes to golf, does God play favorites? If God's gusts blow only for the holy, then how does it explain the golfing prowess of Kim Jong Il, the despotic leader of the rogue nation North Korea.

He's had five aces. All in one round. Yep, on the way to shooting a jaw-dropping thirty-eight-under par thirty-four at the Pyongyang Golf Course, Kim fired five aces on the regulation course, a fact verified by none other than Pyongyang club pro Park Young Nam, who said, "Dear Leader Comrade General Kim Jong Il, whom I respect from the bottom of my heart, is an excellent golfer."

Of course, the Dear Leader's also been known to violate international nuclear treaties and execute foolhardy dissidents (and, presumably, uncooperatively cranky Pyongyang club pros), so maybe a little scorecard chicanery's not out of the question.

But what about Richard M. Nixon? He's one of just three presidents to record an ace and he called it "the greatest thrill of my life—even better than being elected." Why did God elect Nixon to get a hole in one? Because he opened up China? No golfer should ever begrudge a fellow golfer good fortune, but wouldn't you have felt just a bit better for Nixon if he'd used his diplomatic sorcery to open, say, the only slightly less restrictive Augusta National? You can bet the National Organization for Women would have.

A religious man will call it a blessing, a sinner will call it luck. We'll leave it to the theologians and the rabbit's-foot rubbers to debate. But here are some aces and their infectious good fortune in which skill can't take all the credit.

🍀 LUCKY SYMBOL

If while on your way to the golf course you spot a crow on the road, honk your horn at it. If it refuses to move from its spot, some believe you will be granted good luck for the day. Of course, if the crow doesn't fly away, take safe evasive maneuvers or it could be a very unlucky day for the immobile bird.

A One Putt

The Worldwide Hole-in-One Society reports on October 22, 2002, that Fergus Muir scored an ace using a putter at the Eden in St. Andrews. Muir, a 13-handicapper, said he frequently uses his fifty-year-old putter because it gives him more control than even the most modern clubs and, of course, keeps his ball well below the swirling winds. On this blustery day, Muir said he was amazed to watch the ball gingerly skip down the 144-yard fifth fairway and roll into the hole. The St. Andrews Links Trust, which manages the course, says it can't recall anyone ever acing any hole using a putter.

The feat is not without precedent. Ryan Procop was reportedly so disgusted with himself after taking a 12 at the previous hole that he grabbed his putter for his tee shot at the 168-yard par 3 at Glen Eagles Golf Club, Ohio. He aced it.

A Mow-ving Experience

Bob Bacharach had been golfing for forty years without an ace when he dunked two in two months. The second one was at a 138-yard hole at Alondra Golf Club in Torrance, California, and earned a somewhat grudging bow from a long-time buddy, who told him, "Okay, this one I'll give you."

"The guy's a real rules stickler—I am, too—but he didn't believe my first one counted," Bacharach says.

It did. It may have been that some aces turn friends green with envy—John Deere green.

It was at the 191-yard sixteenth hole at Victoria Golf Course in Carson, California. Bacharach hit what he thought was a good shot that looked about a foot away from the cup. The guys in the group said a perfunctory, "Nice shot, Bob." To all eyes from the tee box, it looked like the shot would leave the sixty-two-year-old Bacharach with a feathery little birdie putt.

"We were about eighty yards away and I could still see the ball sitting there—it looked like maybe a foot or so away," Bacharach said. "Just then a maintenance guy on a lawn mower came roaring by about twenty feet behind the green. I guess the vibration dislodged the ball and got it rolling. Anyway, the next thing we know, we look up and the ball's gone. It had dropped right in the hole. An ace!"

Golf Balls Bounce, But Cash Does Not

Harriet Goldstein didn't take up golf for the thrills or the competitive aspects of the game. She did it for more soulful reasons. An administrative assistant for a Boston-area law firm, she wanted to golf to enjoy the outdoors, the socializing, and the camaraderie that comes with shared fun.

"Never in a million years did I think someday I'd get a hole in one," she says.

A million years? Try five.

It was the sixteenth hole at Lakeville Country Club in Lakeville, Massachusetts. Goldstein, fifty-one, judged it a 5 wood. It was straight, but short.

"It's a tricky shot because there's water on both sides," she says. "It was going straight, perfectly straight at the hole and I was hoping it would make it to the green."

The ball was short until—boing!—it hit the cart path and took a kangaroo kick of more than thirty feet high. It landed on the green with enough juice to bounce twice and then, plop, right in the cup. The green fronts the Lakeville clubhouse and on this perfect Memorial Day weekend for golf, the place was packed with excited observers.

Thirsty ones.

"I just went nuts," Goldstein says. "I must have danced for fifteen minutes. There's a house right next to the tee and some guy comes out on his porch and says, 'All right, who had the hole in one?' A bunch of guys from the clubhouse came out and started yelling, 'Take a bow! Take a bow!' It was so happy and unexpected, I'll never forget it as long as I live."

Her luck continued when she got to the clubhouse bar and learned they didn't take credit cards.

LUCKY SYMBOL
"See a penny, pick it up, all day long you'll have good luck." Some office workers in the World Trade Centers on 9/11 reported that they stopped their frantic descents down the steps to pick up fallen pennies. They survived.

"After paying for golf and lunch, all I had was two dollars on me. They'd been setting up drinks for the half hour or so it took us to play the last three holes. The bill must have been close to two hundred dollars, but they didn't take credit cards. They said to just forget about it."

Good Shot, Better Deed

Tim Hovancsek's ace earned him $15,000, but cost him several years of happy devotion. He'd been a teaching pro at an Arizona course in 1989 when he met and worked with Heather Farr, a talented young golfer who was on her way to the LPGA Tour.

Still, Farr's greatest adversary wasn't bunker shots, water hazards, or knee-knocker putts for birdie. She was battling a deadly cancer that in 1993 killed the Arizona State University graduate at the age of twenty-four.

Hovancsek used most of the money to start the "Farr & Above Foundation," a philanthropic organization that raises money for cancer research and promotes junior golf in her name.

"She battled cancer for five years, but still gave of herself," he said. "In 1989, I hosted a junior clinic in Scottsdale for about five hundred kids and Heather was still there helping out. The chemotherapy left her without hair, but she still spent time with the kids talking about life and golf. From that day on, I made it my mission to make a difference. All I needed was a way to make that difference. The money from my ace opened that door."

A Dearly Missed Brother, Three Remarkably Hit Shots

Debbie Lewis had left a lovely flower arrangement for husband Julian. It was October 1, 2002, what would have been his brother Gary's thirty-sixth birthday. Julian looked at the flowers and the sweet note saying she understood he would be down and might be needing a little lift that day.

Maybe, somehow, it was something Gary, too, understood.

"I'd just been laid off the week before from my job as a computer hardware salesman," Julian, forty-one, says. "I looked at the flowers and the note and then went to look at a collage of pictures of Gary. I still miss him."

A day that would begin with so much soulful melancholy would end with euphoria. Michael Burke called to see if Julian wanted to golf on that warm autumn day at the Quail Hollow Golf Club in Concord, Ohio, where both are members. Julian was planning on starting his own business and thought a round of golf might be a good antidote for the weary worries and uncertainties swirling through his life.

He was wrong.

"I wasn't playing well at all," says Lewis, a 10-handicapper. "It was a frustrating round, then we came to the sixteenth."

The 490-yard par 5 offers a nice risk/reward option. It's narrow with OB on the left and fairway-hugging trees right. Catch a sweet bounce and this slightly downhill dogleg left is reachable in two.

Hershey's Chocolates have to labor for years to produce the sort of sweetness that began happening to Lewis over the course of three remarkable shots. His well-struck drive hit, he thinks, maybe a sprinkler head or something that gave it an accelerating bound down the fairway. He was 160 yards from the hole and chose a "7 or 8 iron." The following events understandably blurred his recollections.

"The pin was in the middle of the green. I hit it good, but we couldn't find it. I looked all over the green, the front, and finally in the hole. There it was! I couldn't believe it. I'd made an albatross!"

Albatross. The feat is so rare many golfers don't know that's the old English term for the more regal-sounding double eagle.

The seventeenth is a 140-yard par 3. Want to guess who hit first?

He took a 9 iron. It had a slight draw to it, and hit five inches behind the flag and bounced back to snuggle between the stick and the cup.

"I started shaking and trembling. I'd never had a double eagle and I'd never had a hole in one. You can say one's really lucky, but for both of them to happen on consecutive holes, to me, that goes way beyond luck. When I got the ace, I said, 'Thanks, Gary, I know you must have had something to do with this.'"

A Truly Surgical Swing

George Jensen had been golfing ace-free for fifty years. A decorated World War II Army veteran, Jensen, seventy-nine, had earned his medals at Okinawa and throughout the bloody fighting in the South Pacific. He keeps them in an honored place in the Cozad home where he and his wife, Darlene, raised their four children.

A grateful U.S. government gave him those medals. He got some metals from a hostile Japanese army that he carried with him.

"He never complained, but he was in a lot of pain," says Darlene.

The shrapnel began taking a toll and soon an army of surgeons tried to restore him to a pain-free life with which to enjoy his ten grandchildren, all of whom, like their parents, enjoy golf.

"He had five bypasses and three back surgeries," says Darlene, a non-golfer who still enjoys riding along with the family. "The last time they told us they couldn't promise us that he'd ever be able to walk again. It was scary."

Doctors at Exempla Lutheran Medical Center in Denver installed even more hardware: two rods, bolts, nuts, fastening screws—don't be surprised if X rays show a wristwatch or two.

But walk, he did. He walked practically straight back to the golf course that had given him so much joy. Then in May 2002, after all that surgery, he had his first ace at the 111-yard par 3 fifteenth hole at Cozad Country Club, where he golfs nearly every afternoon.

It happened again on the same hole just four months later. Each time the Cozad State Bank's sent him a $50 congratulatory bond, and he's starting to make the bank board members a tad nervous.

"The second one he said was the greatest thrill of his life," Darlene said. "To us, it's really a miracle. We can't explain it. He'd been golfing fifty years and then to get one after all that

🍀 **LUCKY SIGN**
An old German folk belief is that if a man riding overland on a horse comes across a woman spinning, then it is a very bad sign and the man should turn and find another way. For modern golf purposes, if a man riding an EZ-Go golf cart comes across a woman spinning then in all likelihood he's come across a stag golf tournament.

surgery in which they said he might never even walk again, well, it just amazes you."

It may be a drastic solution, but if you've tried everything else and still haven't had your ace, you might want to schedule some back surgery at the Exempla Lutheran Medical Center in Denver.

It worked wonders for Jensen.

Amen . . . Yippee! Yippee Again!

Like many veteran golfers, Evelyn Tucci's prayer was a common one: "I prayed that before I died, I'd get a hole in one," she says.

A 32-handicapper who rarely breaks 100, Tucci got her first ace on the 112-yard second hole at the Crystal Lake Country Club in Pompano Beach, Florida. She got her second just three holes later on the 157-yard fifth hole. Both were stuck with her trusty 4 wood.

Maybe she's more devout than other golfers who've been uttering the same prayer heavenward for many, many years. Or maybe it's just that she's been more persistent and patient. In either case, she had waited long enough.

Tucci was eighty-two when she had her big day.

Holy Smokes!

The Reverend Harold Snider had golfed his entire life up through the morning of June 9, 1975, without ever having an ace. By the time he went to bed that night he had three. The first was at the eighth hole of the Ironwood course near Phoenix. The other two happened at the 110-yard thirteenth hole, and the 135-yard fourteenth. Ironwood is a par 3 course, but there's nothing artificial about that kind of sharp shooting.

"Who Do You Have to Know to Get Really Lucky?"

Dale Wilbur heard the sheepish prayers. May have been even tempted to utter one himself.

"I know a lot of golfers pray God will let them get a hole in one before they die," he says. "I know a lot of golfers pray when they're standing over a five-foot putt for birdie to win a match. I tell them God has a lot more to worry about than their golf game."

He's right. It's all there in the headlines. War, famine, violence, "Minister Wins Hole-in-One Contest . . ."

Huh?

Yup. That was the headline in the local papers the day Wilbur, the music minister at the First Baptist Church in Georgetown, Texas, aced to win a $20,000 Chevy truck or the cash equivalent, which he accepted on behalf of his church. He'd been golfing thirty-two years and had attended college on a golf scholarship. A former club champion, he'd never had an ace.

"It's funny because we were in a fund-raiser for the Children at Heart Golf Marathon where teams play a 100-holes-in-a-day marathon."

He had thought he and playing partner Jerry Mullins would each have an opportunity to go for the hole-in-one prize on the eighth hole at Berry Creek Country Club, but Mullins informed him on the way to the course that only one could go.

"I told Jerry I wanted him to take it, but he said no, I should," Wilbur says. "We went back and forth, but he persuaded me to take it."

Good thing. When it went in, Wilbur confesses to "running around, laughing and screaming" and generally carrying on like a sailor out for a four-day sin binge. That same week, another parishioner at his church, Buford Powell, won a Buick

LaSabre for acing a hole at another event, and soon lifelong Presbyterians were considering attending First Baptist. A religious conversion would be a small price to pay to get an ace, it was said.

"Yeah, that was the joke," Wilbur says. "'Go to First Baptist and get a hole in one.' It was a great way for me to spread the word of God, golf always is. But, really, I think I'm a better witness for Him when I hit a bad shot, rather than a good one. That's when people really watch to see how a man of God behaves."

Religious Hole in One

Moses, Jesus, and an old man are golfing. Moses steps up to the tee and hits the ball. It goes sailing over the fairway and lands in the water. Moses parts the water and chips the ball onto the green.

Jesus steps up to the tee and hits the ball. It goes sailing over the fairway and lands in the water. Jesus walks on the water, takes a deep swing, and chips the ball onto the green.

The old man steps up to the tee and hits the ball. It goes sailing over the fairway and heads for the water. But just before it falls into the water, a fish jumps up and grabs the ball in its mouth. As the fish is falling back into the water, an eagle swoops down and grabs the fish in its claws. The eagle flies over the green where a lightning bolt shoots from the sky and barely misses it. Startled, the eagle drops the fish. When the fish hits the ground, the ball pops out of his mouth and rolls into the cup for a hole in one.

Jesus turns to the old man and says, "Dad, if you don't stop showing off, next time we won't bring you."

Beginner's Luck . . . Finally!

REVENGE, IT IS SAID, is a dish that is best served cold. How about an ace? Which offers the sweeter sensation: achieving the perfect shot on the first swing during your first round or waiting more than five bewildering decades to get the shot that's spent a lifetime eluding your scorecard?

For most golfers the answer is either/or. Most golfers aren't greedy. They'd just like to say that at one time in their life they got a hole in one, just to see what it's like, to know how it feels, and, yes, to rub it in on the rest of us who've never gotten even one.

Here are some aces that remind us that golf's hole in one, at its heart, is a tease. It can precociously seduce you with the very first swing or it can play hard to get through a lifetime of frustrating stick nicks before finally acknowledging your flirtation by sticking its tongue down your throat when you least expect it.

Hot Shot Tot

Jack Nicklaus says kids are ready for golf when they reach an age when they can resist the urge to stop chasing frogs on the fairways. Jake Paine was probably still tempted to go after the aquatic hoppers, but then he'd already accomplished by the age of three what some golfers spend a lifetime chasing: a hole in one.

In August 2001, Paine was playing the Lake Forest Golf and Practice Course in Lake Forest, California. The sixth hole is a 66-yard uphill hole that proves difficult for many golfers. But for Jake, the hole was mere child's play.

"Daddy, I got a hole in one!" he exclaimed.

He was playing with his father, Bill Paine, and his brother, Jordan, seven. Golfer Joe Zamberlan was on a nearby hole. The trio witnessed what is considered to be the youngest golfer to score a hole in one.

"It was a Tiger shot," said Jake, from Rancho Santa Margarita, referring to his hero, Tiger Woods. "I'm happy."

The three-foot-two ace used a Snoopy driver, which is thirty inches high, just about up to the thirty-five-pound-boy's chin. Zamberlan, who was playing the adjacent number five hole, saw the ball bounce left and fall into the hole.

"I was shocked," said Zamberlan. "I ran over and asked how old he was. I can't even birdie that hole."

Jake, who'd been golfing since he turned two years old, went on to shoot a 48 on the nine-hole, par-29 course.

The rest of the day was spent posing for pictures for local newspapers and television, and proving the shot was no fluke. When asked to take a few swings for the camera, he stepped up to the tee and plunked one down on the same green only a few feet from the cup.

Jake was exactly three years, five months, and fifteen days old.

The age shattered youngest hole-in-one records that had been posted by various five-year-olds throughout the world. As recently as 1999, *Golf Digest* listed six-year-old Keith Long of Seline, Michigan, as having the youngest ace.

Local reporters for the *Orange County Register* tracked down the parents of another local golfer of some renown to find out when he'd first hit a hole in one. Mr. and Mrs. Earl Woods told reporters that their boy, Eldrick, didn't ace until he was the ripe old age of six, and that it happened at the Heartwell Golf Course in Long Beach, and while they didn't recall which hole it was, they remembered that it was 105 yards long and that Tiger used a 3 wood.

Jake may have called it a "Tiger shot," but Woods was twice Jake's age before he hit one like Jake did. For a competitive golfer like Woods, that's one Painful reminder of at least one record he'll never hold.

ACE CANDY BAR
The nutritional information on a "Hole in One" energy bar reveals that the chocolate and peanut butter treat contains just 6 grams of fat.

The Boy Wonder

Nicholas Parker-Gregory is a Tour veteran. He's the son of LPGA player Kristal Parker-Manzo and golf instructor Jim Gregory and knows professional golf the way fish know water.

He entered the record books on February 2, 2002, when he used a 7 iron to ace the 55-yard second hole at the Family Golf Center's Orange Course in Mesa, Arizona. He was just three years, two months old.

The toddler's been traveling with his mom and has been swinging a club since he was just sixteen months old, says Parker-Manzo.

"I take him to the range after my rounds and let him hit balls," she says. "He always draws a crowd. He doesn't realize how special what he did is. To him, the important thing is that he beat his grandparents on the hole."

All Downhill From There

Friends in Bill Griffith's barbershop coaxed Bill Higginbotham of Terre Haute, Indiana, to tag along for a round of golf at Linton Municipal one day in March 1963, despite his protestations that he'd never even swung a club. Still when it came time for Higginbotham to hit, he did something that's still barbershop fodder wherever hairs are scissored. Using a borrowed 7 iron, he aced the first hole the first time he'd ever swung a club.

What's So Tricky About That?

Trick shot artist Paul Hahn was barnstorming the Midwest in 1965 when a kid named Jim Haderer at West Park Golf Course in Elgin, Illinois, stepped up and said, "Hey, I'd like to try that."

Hahn had just been down on his knees whacking balls to a green 190 yards out. It wasn't uncommon for those in the audience to attempt Hahn's gags. What happened next was.

Haderer, sixteen, got down on his knees and, on his very first try, put the ball straight into the cup.

So That's How It's Done

It took one exhilarating shot to get Darci Fulford hooked on golf. She was playing with her parents on the 110-yard sixth hole at Plainfield (New Jersey) Country Club with the goal of actually doing something she'd never before achieved in golf: finish out a hole. She did it in one stroke.

Using her father's 7 iron, she aced, truly a fantastic finish.

Her parents had been golfing for a combined total of forty years and between them had never celebrated an ace.

Ace and Out

On a scorecard that could only please a bored mathematician with a broken calculator, David Terpoilli of West Norristown, Pennsylvania, wrote a "1" at the 128-yard sixteenth hole on his way to shooting, gulp, 123-over 193 at Whitemarsh Country Club in October 1994. The scorecard's back nine reads: 9-21-9-16-11-13-1-11-9=100.

The beauty of it is that no one who ever wrote "21" for one hole could ever be accused of lying about his ace five holes later.

Terpoilli told *Sports Illustrated*'s Jack McCallum in 1997 that he quit golf that day.

"I haven't picked up a club since. How could I ever top that?"

A Charm

In 1977, a fourteen-year-old named Gillian Field took a number of lessons and aced the tenth hole at Moor Place Golf Course near London. It was the first time she'd ever set foot on a golf course.

Something Must Be Wrong

Dick Groat's enjoyed some of the greatest thrills collegiate and professional sports offer. He's a two-time basketball All-American from Duke and was college player of the year in 1951. A two-sport superstar long before Deion Sanders purchased his first earring, Groat won the National League MVP as shortstop for the Pittsburgh Pirates in 1960 and won World Series rings with both the Pirates in 1960 and the St. Louis Cardinals in 1964.

He never had an ace until he was playing at a recent scramble at Nemacolin Country Club in Farmington, Pennsylvania, a short drive from Ligonier where Groat lives and owns Champion Lakes Golf Course, one of the finest public courses in the state.

"The great part about that was (former Pirate teammate and broadcaster) Nellie King had just marked a closest-to-the-pin from about 3 feet and he stood there and watched me erase his great shot with a hole in one," Groat says.

"Funny thing was, there was this young girl there helping out at the tournament. She came up to me later and seemed sort of upset. She said, 'Mr. Groat, I stood there all afternoon and I didn't see another one. Yours was the only one out there all day.' She seemed to think it's something that happens all the time and that I was the only one who'd actually done it the way it was supposed to be done. It was my first ace."

An Ace Trumps a Résumé

Gregg Greenberg was a recent graduate of the Cornell School of Business with two things on his mind when attending a local job fair: He wanted a job and all the free stuff he could get his hands on. That's why Greenberg, a non-golfer, didn't hesitate to snag a free golf ball with a spiffy Aramark corporate logo emblazoned on the side.

The ball was gathering dust when some friends called with a novel idea: Hey, why don't you take that golf ball and come play a round with us?

"I'd golfed maybe three times in my life, but I didn't have anything really going on so I said, sure, golf, why not?"

He doesn't remember much about the details that are etched for eternity on the souls of other golfers. He doesn't remember the hole, the exact yardage, or the green speed that day. He does clearly remember the club he selected, and it wasn't a decision that taxed his bright young mind.

"Oh, yeah," he says. "It was a 3 iron. I remember taking that because it's the only club I can hit straight."

And straight is where he hit it that day at the Robert Trent Jones course in Ithaca, New York. He sort of bladed it, but that didn't matter in the result.

"It went right in the hole. Right in. The guys I was playing with were real serious golfers who were keeping real score and they were furious. They were cussing me the whole day because neither of them had ever had a single ace," he recalls with a diabolical chuckle.

He took that lucky Aramark ball and called the recruiter who'd given it to him. He told him that he'd used the ball to score a hole in one and that he wanted to work for Aramark.

"I said I was feeling lucky and was going to fax him my résumé and then hit the casinos. I remember I lost between three hundred to four hundred dollars that night."

They liked his initiative and invited him to their Philadelphia offices intent on luring the young man to work for them. Took him out to dinner at a swanky joint. Took him to a 76ers game. Great seats. Offered him a job for $55,000 a year.

"I tell you what, that ace got me a great night in Philadelphia, but I waited around and wound up taking a better job for more money. I did get a great story out of it and now, I can always say I've had a hole in one. Haven't played another round since 1998."

> ♣ **PAR 3 PRAYER**
> *"Please, Lord, let me prove to all my friends and enemies that a hole in one won't spoil me."*

First Time's a Charm

You can't call Steve Thorwald, a retired advertising agent, a beginner. No, the man's a certified member of the Golf Nut Society (#0476) and has been devoted to the game for years. In fact, he's had eight aces. It wasn't Thorwald, sixty-one, who enjoyed the beginner's luck.

It was his club.

"I'd been looking for a good wedge and found this one at Fiddler's Greens, a golf store near my home in Eugene, Oregon," he says. "It was a Cleveland Tour Action with a forty-eight-degree loft. I picked that thing up in the store and, man, it just felt perfect. Took it with me the next day to golf with some friends at the Springfield Country Club."

The 130-yard third hole provided an opportunity to see if the club that could talk the talk could actually walk the walk.

"I was telling the guys just how great this club felt," he says. "I mean perfect. I told them I'd never even swung it before, but it just felt great."

After one swing, that Cleveland Tour Action was batting 1.000. Thorwald aced.

After that it was all downhill and today the club's gathering dust in the Thorwald garage.

"I don't recall what it was, but it must have done something wrong to earn banishment to the garage," Thorwald said.

Golfers are a remorseless bunch.

＞ ●

Burdens Lifted, Ball Dropped

Eddie Randolph doesn't recommend it for everyone, but he thinks leaving a job helped him get an ace. He'd retired after forty-two years as a district plant manager for the local school district. He'd been golfing forty-six of his sixty-one years, too, and had enjoyed nearly all the thrills golf has to offer. He'd caddied for hockey great Gordie Howe, golf great Sam Snead, and baseball great Al Kaline. As for himself, he once carried an 8 handicap.

"I figured I'd done about everything I could in golf, but have my ball go in the hole on a par 3. Never had an ace. And it gnawed at me."

So did having to work for a living. Sure, he liked the people and the job security, but even the happiest employee should never forget that the biblical man who had more misery befall him spelled his name J-O-B.

Coincidence? Probably not.

Randolph retired on August 31, 2001. The next day he got his ace.

It was at the 163-yard sixth hole at the Plum Hollow Golf Course in South Field, Michigan.

"To tell you the truth, it does feel different golfing as a retired person," he says. "I've played thousands of par 3s, but to be standing there as a retired person made a world of difference. Maybe I was more positive or more content. Either way, I got my ace."

His buddies were there to watch, too. Tom Conti, Tom Denomme, and, cruelly, Al Napolitano, who's been the card-signing witness for all three of his friends' aces. And he's never had one.

"Yeah, we kid him about it. It's all good-natured, but it gets to him. But we can't help it! I ask everyone I meet if they've heard about my hole in one and ever since I've started signing all my stuff 'Ace.'"

Golf's Purple Heart

The Redan Hole (fifteenth) at the North Berwick's West Links Course is one of the most difficult par 3s in the world and one of the most architecturally copied. The hole was named after defensive fortifications employed by the Russian Army during the Crimean War (1853–56), when dashing Russian General Prince Menschikoff and his boys gave the Allied British, French, and Turkish forces a stout beating.

The Brits could have used a man with the patience and persistence of honorable Robert Aitken of Westerdunes Park, England. He'd been playing golf for sixty years, since he was just ten years old, and twice a week since 1949. He'd never had an ace.

Then in November 2001, Aitken, seventy, teed it up on the Redan where the bunkers are positioned to represent the attacking forces. Aitken deployed a 5 iron and attacked the 192-yard hole from the back tees.

Victory!

"I didn't actually see the ball go in, but when I went up to the green it was in the hole," he said. "I do play regularly, but I have never hit a hole in one before so it was a nice feeling."

Sixty Years Between Bulls'-Eyes

Arthur Mills learned to play target golf when he was going after some more strategically important targets than golf holes. He picked up the game in his spare time in Europe between piloting B-24 bombing runs over the Polesti oil fields in Romania, the largest oil reserves available to European fascists bent on conquering the world. The fields were surrounded by deadly defenses that had claimed the lives of many Allied fighters and comrades of Retired Colonel Mills.

"I flew fifty missions over Polesti," he says. "I was never shot down, but my copilot had his arm nearly shot off from a bullet that went right through my window."

Given the feverish activity of his "day" job, it's understandable that a man like Mills would be drawn to the pastoral pleasures offered by a round of golf. He took to the game and as a civilian worked to drop his handicap, an infinitely more satisfying pursuit than being shot at while trying to drop angry explosives.

He got to be pretty good, too. His handicap descended to a 5, but the one golf thrill that eluded him was the hole in one.

"Oh, I'd been close too many times to count, but I just never got one. Really, I didn't think I ever would."

Still, he'd always enjoyed golf, flying, and was happy to have made it through World War II intact enough to enjoy both. In fact, as his eightieth birthday approached, Colonel

Mills still enjoyed flying and eagerly accepted an invitation to jet from his Collierville, Tennessee, home to Boca Raton, Florida, where a commercial charter company he once owned still invited him down to fly some new winged wonders. On September 3, 2001, he eagerly accepted just such an invitation and flew down in such a hurry he forgot his clubs and the golf glasses he wears to correct a nagging anti-astigmatism that deprives him of vision of more than 100 feet.

But what he lacked in equipment he more than made up for in enthusiasm. When friends asked the Mills if he had time to tee it up at Boca Del Mar Country Club, his answer was affirmative.

It was at the fifth hole that the seventy-nine-year-old veteran finally struck the target for which he'd been aiming for sixty years.

"I couldn't see the green," he says. "I just heard the guys I was playing with yell, 'Hit it! Hit it! . . . It's in the hole!' All those years of golfing, I'd never had one—never even seen one. Finally, I get one and I didn't get to see it. Still, what a thrill!"

Patience Is a Virtue. So Is Longevity

Harold Stilson was seventy years old before he got his first ace in the game he took up when he was twenty. He remembered they gave him a plaque. He got squat for the next four, but people sure made a fuss when he knocked in his sixth, a 4 iron on the 108-yard sixteenth hole at Deerfield Country Club at his home in Deerfield Beach, Florida.

ESPN broadcast the news on *SportsCenter* the next day back in May 2001. Jay Leno and Regis called, too. Deerfield club president Ken Knight had to call a press conference to deal with all the media requests.

Stilson was surprised at all the commotion. "For God's sake! For a hole in one!"

You betcha. Stilson, you see, was born in the shadow of the turn of the century. Not this one. The last century.

Born April 10, 1900, when William McKinley—who?—was president of these forty-five United States. Oklahoma, Arizona, New Mexico, Alaska, and Hawaii all gained admission to the Union after Stilson did.

He was born in history to someday himself achieve it. He did it by breaking a record that had stood fifteen years—a ninety-nine-year-old man named Otto Butcher of Switzerland had aced at La Manga Golf Course in Spain.

Stilson's fifth ace came when he, too, was a still-spry ninety-nine, but he was sixty days shy of Butcher's ancient age. To beat it, Stilson would need precious amounts of time and luck.

He got both.

He never saw the ace that landed him in the record books. He hit the ball, saw it was going straight, and walked away without watching it.

"Someone said, 'Uh, oh. I think it's coming pretty close,'" Stilson said. "Then they said, 'It went in!'"

To Stilson, he couldn't understand why anyone cared. "Eh, so it's a hole in one," he said with a shrug. "A hole in one is just a ball that's struck well that has a little luck going in."

Stilson had a little luck going in. He's in the record books, a fact that was much remarked upon at his funeral February 2, 2002, as was his often offered secret to a long life: Drink beer and eat a lot of popcorn.

So as you go through life, oldest ace is one record every golfer should shoot for. First you have to get there. Because in golf, one of your very first goals is to break 100.

With a little luck, you can make it one of your last.

ACE JOKE

Robert and Charlie go golfing every Saturday. One Saturday, he comes home three hours late. His wife asks him, "What took you so long?"

Robert says, "That was the worst day of golf I've ever had. We got to the first tee and Charlie hit a hole in one and immediately dropped dead of a heart attack."

Robert's wife says, "That's terrible!"

Robert says, "You're telling me. Then for the rest of the round, it was, hit the ball, drag Charlie, hit the ball, drag Charlie, hit the ball . . ."

Fathers, Sons, Family Affairs

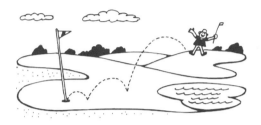

THE ACT OF GOLFING is a selfish one. It's you against the course, your only ally being your practiced swing, and there are times when that coward should be stood against a wall and shot for desertion. It's just you and your swing standing over that smug, tauntingly stoic white ball and acres and acres of hazards waiting to ruin your day

But, really, the serious part of golf—addressing the ball and swinging at it—shouldn't take more than twelve seconds. That means a golfer taking 100 strokes during any four-hour thirty-minute, eighteen-hole round is going to require twelve hundred seconds or twenty minutes to actually golf. The remainder of that time is generally spent in carefree conversation, lighthearted banter, and trying to time various barnyard noises to occur during your opponent's backswing.

That's what many golfers love about the game: the four hours and ten minutes spent while waiting to swing a club. It's the camaraderie, the fellowship, the escape from stressful endeavors. And that's why golfing together is often an important day on any family calendar.

Many of us were lucky enough to learn the game at the

knees of our fathers or other caring loved ones. A round of golf with a casual friend can be a joyful occasion. A round with a father, a brother, a mother, a sister, a son, a daughter, or a grandchild is a memory to treasure for a lifetime.

An ace shared with one of them is priceless enough to make a pagan feel blessed.

Copy Cats

The Brownson Country Club in Shelton, Connecticut, had hosted countless rounds to the Curran boys without ever giving up a single ace. Then in the summer of 2001, it began to relent. One by one, hole by hole.

"I'd been golfing more than forty-five years and had never had an ace—none of us had," says Tom Curran, Sr., sixty-eight. "I've rolled him by, had 'em stop an inch or two from the hole, but never had one drop. Same goes for my boys. Not Tom Junior, not James, not Chris, and not Mike."

The dam broke, fittingly, by the man who'd been frustrated the longest.

"It was the seventeenth hole," he says. "It's uphill, 150 yards. Blind. I used a 7 iron. I didn't see it go in, but that didn't make it any less special. We got up there and looked in the hole and there it was. It was everything I'd dreamed it would be."

None of his sons was there to share the joy. Fate had other plans.

Within thirty-nine days, Tom Junior had aced the par 3 fifth hole and Chris came through with one on number six to win a trip to the Curran family's ancestral Irish homeland.

"These kids are always copying me," he says. "Anything I did, they had to do, too."

So Good, So Young

John Francis is a 3-handicapper and a man who was just 22 yards shy of hitting the longest, but may have hit what is arguably the greatest double eagle in golf history. It happened in 1989 at a 625-yard hole at Skyland Country Club in Crested Butte, Colorado.

"I hit that second shot and, man, it really had some steam on it," Francis says. "It was so far away I couldn't see it, but I saw the maintenance guys in the back of the green going crazy. I got up there and they told me it hit on the fly. It broke the back of the cup and stayed in."

Still, it may be a bigger thrill for him every time he watches his thirteen-year-old son Philip put a tee in the ground on the first hole. That simple act is usually followed by amazing feats. The Scottsdale, Arizona, youth has won four Junior World Championships in a row and is hailed as a prodigy by famed golf teacher Jim Flick, who was told by a fatherly sounding Jack Nicklaus, "Don't try to make him too perfect," Flick said. "I'm not, really, but you couldn't tell it by looking. He understands the swing as well as any Tour player and he's a boy who still loves learning."

Nicklaus told John Francis, "Just give him the opportunities he needs to succeed and stay out of his way," Francis recalls. "And that's just what I'm doing. Nothing this kid does surprises me. He's got this quiet confidence. He rarely speaks about kicking someone's butt, but he's like Oscar de la Hoya. He's quiet on the golf course, but he wants blood. He doesn't care if its his own mother, he wants blood. He's got his own agenda. He's already figuring out who he wants to fly his corporate jet. He's only thirteen years old, but he believes he'll be better than anybody who ever lived."

The only time Francis has seen Philip show any fist-pumping emotion on a golf course is when he aces. His dad's seen three of his six.

"He's real quiet, but a hole in one really sets him off," Francis says. "It just sets him off. It's the only time I see any reaction from him. I think it's because he expects himself to play well, but no one expects the ball to go right in the hole."

Sports Illustrated said John and Birgitta's son may be the most accomplished golfer at his age in history.

Who said John's never had an ace?

Clearly, he's raising one.

For Uncle Joe

Joe Fialla didn't begin golfing until he turned fifty. He was going to put it off until he retired from Verizon Wireless, where he works as a network planner, but friends said it's good to learn the game with "new bones."

Today, three years later, he's yet to break 100 and he may never.

But, as he's quick to point out, he does have a hole in one. Quick to point it out? Compared to Fialla, new grandparents are glacial in gushing about their offspring.

"Oh, yeah," he says. "I've got a guy I work with and he's a 3-handicapper who's been golfing twenty-eight years. With him, I really rub it in."

And why not? When the ball was in the air above the sixth hole at The Ponds at Lake Grove on Long Island, the Massapequa Park man remembers rejoicing, "Wow! I think I've actually hit the green!"

Better than that. It bounced a time or two and rolled in

the cup. His daughter, Chris, and her husband, Brian Cusati, were watching with disbelieving eyes.

"My son-in-law said, 'What the heck was that?' It was a hole in one! My best score ever is a 105. I don't know whether he had anything to do with it, but I dedicated the ace to my uncle Joe Fialla. He was like a second father to me. I wish he could have been there. Who knows? Maybe he was."

After You, Dear

About the only thing Elaine and Dick Sauers could possibly have had to fight about on this day on May 24, 1998, at the Wolferts Roost Country Club in Albany, New York, was who was going to pick up the dinner check. Elaine used a 7 wood to ace the tenth hole from the 155-yard ladies' tee for her first hole in one. She carded the ace just three hours after her husband, Dick, had done it on the same hole with a 6 iron from 166 yards out. It was his second hole in one.

An Ace for Father's Day

It's a Father's Day tradition to watch the U.S. Open with Dad. If you're lucky, you're sharing a den or family room, but it doesn't make it any less special to sit states apart and enrich the phone companies with every thrilling shot.

Johnny Miller enjoyed a Father's Day from his NBC anchor booth that brought a lump to the throats of golfing fathers all over the world.

His son, Andy, aced the 205-yard third hole with a 5 iron during the final round at the Open at Bethpage Black. The ace caught the usually eloquent and thoughtful anchor momentarily speechless as producers kept replaying the thrilling moment.

"Man, it doesn't get any better than this," he said.

It left Andy so exhilarated that he wasn't thinking too clearly, he admitted. Instead of gift-wrapping the ball and tossing it to his father, Andy threw it—only the thirty-sixth ace to be recorded in U.S. Open history—to the happy and thirsty crowd that had begun chanting, "It's Miller time! It's Miller time!"

"I just picked it up and said why not throw it [into the gallery]," Andy said. "To make a hole in one on Sunday at the U.S. Open—not too many guys get that opportunity. It was unbelievable."

The ace had followed a fine shot from Stuart Appleby, who had been enthusing with his caddie about being just a few feet away for a sure birdie.

"I had a 5 iron and got it close," Appleby said. "I'm talking about my shot because I thought it was a pretty good one. Then he turns around and sticks it."

Johnny Miller had recorded one of his twenty-two aces during the 1982 U.S. Open at Pebble Beach.

Unlike Andy's first ace, this one had plenty of witnesses. His first was like a popular USGA commercial in which a lonely boy cards an ace with only a smiling maintenance worker as a witness.

Father and son were often separated on Father's Day because of the senior Miller's commitment to broadcasting duties. Now, Andy Miller intends to be sure he spends Father's Day with Dad no matter where it is.

More shots like that and their togetherness is all but assured.

Way to Go, Dad!

Retiree Phil Manas, eighty, never saw his first and only ace go in the cup at the eighth hole at Colony West Golf Course in Tamarac, Florida. Neither did his son, Steve, who likely would have needed a spy satellite to view the shot. Steve was home in New Jersey, where he works in public relations for Rutgers, the State University of New Jersey.

It didn't matter. Both of them went nuts.

"The newspaper wrote a story with a headline, 'The Best Shot He Never Saw,'" Phil says. "I never took a lesson and never expected I'd get a hole in one. It was really exciting. Just to walk up there and find the ball in the hole—what a thrill!"

As excited as he was, he thinks Steve was even more manic.

"I called and told him and he yelled and laughed," Phil says. "I really think he was more excited for me than I was — and that's saying something."

Take That, You Waltons!

The Waltons are the epitome of televised family closeness, but they've nothing on the Fribley family of Pana, Illinois. Three generations of Fribleys have aced the same hole.

It all started with Grandpa John Fribley. The sixty-five-year-old used a 3 wood to ace the 186-yard seventh hole at Pana Country Club. Four years later, his grandson, Scott, sixteen, did the same. It took sixteen years, but the generation gap was finally bridged by Judge Joseph Fribley—John's son and Scott's father—who used a 4 iron to become the third generation to get one on lucky number seven.

Don't Look Back, She's Catching Up . . . Fast

Most successful marriages are built around shared understanding. Not when it comes to holes in one.

A wall in Jack and Phyllis Bueche's home in the Pocket Area of Sacramento has revered room for all the family aces. In a forty-five-year golfing career, Jack has six balls mounted from his six aces, including the two he made in six days. He's also had a double eagle.

Poor Phyllis had just had one and it tended to get lost amid the clutter of her husband's gaudy luck. One October day in 2000, she began to stake her claim to the need to expand the family trophy room.

It happened on the heavily bunkered sixteenth hole, a 125-yard par 3, at Valley Hi Country Club. Jack was there, and so were friends Bob and Diane Ayres. They all saw her ball apparently land in the sand trap.

"I hit a 6 iron," Phyllis said. "We were looking all over for it. I was looking in a sand trap when Bob and Diane told me, 'We found your ball. It's in the hole!'"

The course was closed the next day, but the day after Phyllis showed up to meet friends for a best ball tournament. This time the sand did not come into play. In fact, little but the bottom of the cup did.

"My friend [Marilyn Hospman] told me, 'Your ball went in!'" Phyllis said. "I said, 'That's impossible. I just hit a hole in one here Sunday.' It was absolutely unbelievable. It took a couple of hours to sink in."

In just two days, she'd cut her husband's lead in ace totals in half, something that had Jack feeling nervous.

"For her to get two in consecutive rounds means I'm going to have to get busy and get out to the driving range," Jack said. "She's breathing down my neck now. It felt more amazing to me than it did to her. I've been playing for a long time and I've never heard of anything like that happening. It's like being struck by lightning—twice."

A single stroke of lightning burns at about 55,000 degrees Fahrenheit. Ouch.

What happened to Phyllis Bueche can only be described with a word from the extreme opposite reading on the thermometer.

Very cool.

So Who's the Real Player?

He's one of the most illustrious golfers in the history of the game. He's won nine majors, dozens of professional tournaments, and has helped elevate the popularity of golf around the world. Still, there in the annals of hole-in-one lore, the man will always be known as Mr. Vivienne Player.

Gary Player may have carded eighteen aces, but his wife has done something he's never done. She's had two in one round, and came within inches of getting a third.

It was nearly twenty years ago at the Wanderers Golf Course in Johannesburg, South Africa. She was playing with two other ladies when it started to rain on the par 3 seventh tee.

"I hit my shot and then quickly dove under my caddie's umbrella to stay dry," she says. "I said, 'I think I hit a good shot,' and the caddie says, 'Well, I think it's in the hole!' And when we got up there, it was."

Rain wasn't the only thing that would fall from the sky that day. There was a veritable shower of aces. Three holes later she was still accepting congratulations when she hit, egads, another ace.

"I actually saw this one go in the hole from the tee so that was very exciting," she says. "My mother was there that day and she kept getting word through the grapevine that her daughter was getting these aces. She just couldn't believe it."

Amazingly, on the second to last hole, she came within a couple of inches of canning a third ace.

"I got home and called Gary and said, 'Let's see you beat that!'"

He didn't and he still hasn't, but the challenge is issued on a near weekly basis, Mr. Player admits.

"That day I would have given anything to have called my wife and told her I'd just matched her, but I never have. It's something she keeps reminding me of nearly every week of my life."

A Family Affair

The Jubelier family doesn't own the Squaw Creek Country Club in Vienna, Ohio. They just own the ninth hole. It's theirs to do with as they please.

If they built a monumental tower to themselves astride the hole, none of the other members would object. Who could? You don't tug on Superman's cape and when it comes to the ninth hole at Squaw Creek, you don't mess with Harry and Natalie or their two sons, Mark and Steven.

The club wisely allowed the installation of a discreet plaque near the ninth tee informing each and every golfer that the 135-yard hole belongs to the family foursome from the nearby border-hugging Pennsylvania town of Sharon.

Assistant pro Mike Ferranti says, "They all play pretty good within their respective handicaps, but there's no explaining what happened to the family on the ninth hole. I've never heard of anything like it."

And it's likely he never will again.

It all began back in 1970 when Mark was a sixteen-year-old amateur coming back from a golf camp in Latrobe, Pennsylvania. He said the camp was not run by Latrobe's famous native son, but some of Arnold Palmer's magic must have stuck to him when he headed home.

"I'd been there for two weeks of intensive golf training," Mark says. "I learned just enough so that I would embarrass myself. I remember I was playing with Dad that day. I didn't use a tee. Just tossed the ball on the grass. Dad wasn't even watching. He was reaching into his own golf bag when my ball landed next to the stick, bounced once or twice and rolled right in. The hole sits right in front of the clubhouse and a lady friend of ours came out screaming, 'It went in! It went in!'"

Mark remembers feeling a mixture of euphoria and disappointment that the club wouldn't bend the rules so a lucky kid could have a sip of beer.

Mom, a 30-handicapper who's never broken 100, got hers in 1993 when she was sixty-five years old. Then came Dad's turn in 1997 during his seventy-seventh year. After that, all eyes turned toward Steven, who was trying hard to dodge the label of family slacker.

Mark says, "We always play a lot of golf together and it came up every time we were on the tee at number nine."

The remarks were good-natured, but edged with impatience.

"C'mon, Steven, at least get it to the green."

"We're waiting . . ."

"It's all up to you. You're the only holdout."

His holdout ended June 20, 2001, when he, too, holed out.

"He called me at work and told me he'd aced it," Mark says. "He was so excited. But I practically hung up on him to call and confirm it with the clubhouse. I'm not going to take the word of that kid brother of mine."

His word was as true as his aim. Steven was actually double lucky. He'd been playing alone that day, but there were credible witnesses to the ace. The LPGA was hosting an event there later that week and tour officials filming promotional interviews saw the ball drop.

"Could you imagine what would have happened if no one had seen it?" Mark asks. "Who would have believed it?"

Who believes it anyway? Even sober witnesses have trouble believing that all four family members could have just four aces among them and that they all came on the same hole.

Says Mark, "It's unique in human history. People see the plaque—'The Hole-in-One Family of Sharon'—with the dates, but still no one believes it. It really is amazing. We talk about it every time we're standing on that tee. But now the pressure's off. We really made our mark."

About the only one who remains unimpressed with the feat is Natalie, the second acer of the family quartet.

"I tell you, the idea that it was something unusual or important would never have occurred to me," she says. "But I guess it's something pretty unusual. Everyone seems to think so."

And, thanks to a simple plaque, everyone always will.

LUCKY SIGN
Multitudes of Mexicans wishing to strike it rich journey to an obscure Tucson, Arizona, shrine to light a candle on the site where a gambler was killed.

Just the Facts

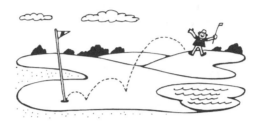

FOR TOO MANY otherwise honest golfers, a good lie has more to do with the permissiveness of the scorekeeper than whether or not the ball comes to rest in an agreeable position. In a revealing 2002 survey by Starwood Hotels & Resorts, 82 percent of 401 high-ranking corporate executives admit to being less than honest on the golf course. They indulge in multiple mulligans, nudge balls away from obstructing trees, and cheerfully shout, "That's five for me," when the scorekeeper saw them take six just to get it to the dance floor.

For Pete's sake, if we can't trust America's corporate executives, men and women to whom we entrust our retirement savings, to be honest, who can we trust?

Golf is the only game where the players police themselves. Honesty and forthrightness are crucial to fair and impartial scoring. So in a land redolent with tax cheats, scofflaws, and court dockets filled to busting, is it any wonder many of golf's most amazing records are tainted with disbelief?

What follows is a timelined list of all relevant hole-in-one records that venerable, rule-finicky organizations like the USGA, the PGA Tour, and *Golf Digest* have said are true. In fairness to the doubters, naysayers, and conspiracy theorists, any doubtful evidence or anecdotally useful information is included so the readers can judge for themselves. Gratuitous, unrelated golf trivia is also sprinkled throughout because, in this age of five-hour weekend rounds, it gives golfers something constructive to talk about while waiting for the leisurely group on the green to plumb bob their two-foot bogie putts.

Remember, the first sentence nearly every golfer hears upon uttering the words, "I just had an ace!" are structured around a word for bovine excrement. This reference chapter is an attempt to cut all that crap out.

Come on In! There's Plenty of Room!

A standard golf ball measures 1.68 inches in diameter. A regulation golf hole measures 4.25 inches in diameter. A golf hole is capable of holding four golf balls at once.

The USGA recommends that a hole in one be considered valid:

(a) If made during a round of at least nine holes, except that a hole in one made during a match should be acceptable even if the match ends before the stipulated round is completed.

(b) If the player is playing one ball; a hole in one made in a practice round in which the player is playing two or more balls should not be acceptable.

(c) If attested by someone acceptable to the committee.

(d) If made at a hole with a temporary tee and/or putting green in use, even if the committee did not specifically define the teeing ground with tee-markers; the length of the hole at the time should be stated on any certificate.

(e) If made in a "scramble" competition, which is played as follows: A side comprises four players. Each member of a side plays from the teeing ground, the best drive is selected, each member plays a second shot from where the best drive is located, and so on.

To paraphrase for the sake of simplicity, for a hole in one to count, it must be witnessed by at least one person willing to sign the scorecard and it must take place on a course with no more than six par 3s. Those are the generally agreed upon criterion for an ace to be deemed worthy.

1869—"Young" Tom Morris, age 17, recorded the first hole in one at Prestwick, number eight, at the Open Championship that September. Numerous sources claim the shot was 166 yards (with some adding "and four inches!"), but the 2003 edition of *The Royal and Ancient Golfer's Handbook* says the shot was 145 yards.

1899—George Grant was issued a patent for the very first golf tee.

1924—First night hole in one was registered by Gene Sarazen at Briarcliff Lodge, Briarcliff Manor, New York. The luminous event occurred during an exhibition in which twenty floodlight projectors and two huge searchlights were activated to illuminate the fairways.

1932—Canadian C. Ross (Sandy) Somerville (1903–91) became the first non-American to win the U.S. Amateur. Two years later, he became the first person of any nationality to record an ace at that uniquely American extravaganza the Masters. Somerville aced number sixteen, the year Horton Smith won the inaugural Masters.

1935—Golf popularity surged when Gene Sarazen double-eagled the par 5 fifteenth hole to catch the leaders at the Masters. The "Shot Heard 'Round the World" propelled him to victory and newsreaders around the world marveled about the odds of anyone hitting a 4 wood 220 yards and having it roll into the cup.

1938—Legendary LPGA golfer Patty Berg won the U.S. Women's Amateur at age twenty after twice finishing runner-up.

1940—In one of the most doggedly determined efforts to make a hole in one, Indiana club pro Harry Gonder teed up a ball at the 160-yard sixteenth hole at his home course, Beverly Shores, Indiana, Country Club. It missed. He spent the next sixteen hours hitting more than 100 balls an hour in a vain attempt to make the ace. His closest shot came on his 1,756 try when his ball stopped one agonizing inch from the cup. He hit another sixty-one shots before giving up in frustration and fatigue. The failure cost him a $25 wager.

1942—The U.S. Open was discontinued for the duration of World War II. A worldwide shortage of rubber, a vital material for freedom-loving fighting forces, created a shortage in the availability and a huge price spike in the cost of golf balls. Sam Snead, a man with a reputation for frugality, played an entire four-day tournament with one golf ball.

1945—Sixteen-year-old Arnold Palmer recorded his third hole in one during a round at Greensburg Country Club. He'd already twice aced the 134-yard second hole at Latrobe Country Club, where his father, Deke, served as greenskeeper and head professional. In 1971, Arnold and Winnie Palmer would purchase the Latrobe Country Club and Palmer would become his father's titular boss.

1947—While paired with Ben Hogan, Claude Harmon became the first of only three players in Masters history to ever ace the diabolically difficult number twelve over Rae's Creek. Hogan's jarringly stoic reaction to the ace became part of golf lore.

1949—Marie Robie of Wollaston, Massachusetts, aced the 393-yard first hole at Furnace Brook Golf Club, on September 4, a female ace distance record that's stood lo these many years.

1951—*Golf Digest* was founded with Bill Davis as editor. Within a year it responded to public appetite for information about golf's mini-miracle, the hole in one, by establishing the National Hole in One Clearinghouse. It would catalog aces until a dearth of sponsorship funding played a role in the magazine's decision to discontinue the effort in 1998.

1954—In twenty years of Masters history, no golfer had ever aced the 190-yard number six hole. That year, two golfers stroked singles here, Leland Gibson and Billy Joe Patton, leaving the 213-yard number four as the only unaced par 3 in the tournament's history. The lonely distinction would remain steadfast for thirty-eight years.

1959—Art Wall, Jr., sank an eleven-foot birdie putt on the seventy-second hole of play at Augusta National to win his only major championship by birdieing five of the last six holes, shooting a 6-under par sixty-six and scoring a one-stroke victory over Jimmy Demaret in one of the most thrilling Masters finishes ever. Wall is considered the Tour champion of aces with forty-six in his career, a total that includes noncompetitive events.

Patty Berg thrilled galleries at the U.S. Women's Open at the 170-yard seventh hole at Churchill Valley Country Club in Pittsburgh. It was the first time any woman had recorded an ace in USGA competition. It was Berg's first and last ace in competitive golf.

1961—On September 4, Richard Nixon, forty-four, became the first president to record an ace, eight years before actually assuming the office. He aced the second hole at the Bel Air Country Club with a 5 iron.

1962—*Golf Digest* proclaimed Dr. Joseph Boydstone for the most prolific stretch of aces known to man. It substantiated Boydstone's claim that he hit eleven aces in one year, including three in one round at Bakersfield Country Club.

In his 1997 article "Ace Venture" for *Sports Illustrated,* Jack McCallum learned that Boydstone, a former physician for the Kern County Jail, had many detractors, including Larry Press, the former sports editor at the *Bakersfield Californian* who lobbied successfully to have Boydstone's alleged ace feats removed from the *World Almanac*. McCallum quoted area pros who said Boydstone was no sharpshooter, but that he was, interestingly, an accomplished hypnotist.

1964—The name Norman Manley of Long Beach, California, made an auspicious and indelible introduction to the roll call of holes in one when he hit the first of fifty-nine reported aces, including, incredibly, two on consecutive par 4s at Del Valle Country Club in Saugus, California. The sheer immensity of his aces has given birth to legions of doubters, but to this day, *Golf Digest* recognizes Manley as the most prolific amateur acer in the history of golf. The magazine's all-time records list published in January 1999 still state that he's the only golfer to ever ace consecutive par 4s.

Tom Cheatwood of Oklahoma City entered the record books by becoming the lefthander who hit the longest ace ever, a 400-yard sweet swipe at the sixth hole at Lake Hefner Golf Club in Oklahoma City.

1965—On the aptly named Miracle Hills Golf Course, Robert Mitera of Omaha hit one "hilluva" miracle that traveled 447 yards and landed in the hole. Although there were no witnesses, *Golf Digest* finds the reports credible enough to still consider it the longest hole in one in American history.

Short game maestro Art Wall set the still-standing record with a 7-under par twenty on the jewel-like par 3 course at the annual tournament preceding the Masters. Gay Brewer matched the record in 1973.

1966—Mancil Davis appeared on the TV game show, *I've Got a Secret* and stumped a foursome panel composed of Bill Cullen, Henry Morgan, Bess Myerson, and Betsy Palmer. The twelve-year-old Odessa, Texas, lad had had eight holes in one and was well on his way to becoming the professional golfer with the most aces, fifty. Today, the "King of Aces" is a highly sought-after golf entertainer who's carded thirteen unofficial aces at corporate outings.

Mrs. William Jenkins, Sr., of Baltimore, Maryland, set the still-standing record for longest double eagle by a woman when she carded an albatross on the 509-yard twelfth hole at Longview Golf Club at Cockeysville, Maryland.

1967—Lew Cullum of Largo, Florida, marked down a nine for an ace at the 145-yard eleventh hole at the Yacht and Estates Golf Club in St. Petersburg, Florida. He sent four consecutive tee shots into the water before finally landing one on the green and into the hole.

1968—Former President Dwight D. Eisenhower aced the thirteenth hole at the Seven Lakes Country Club, an executive course in Palm Springs, California.

1969—Harbour Town Golf Links at Hilton Head, South Carolina, opened. The Pete Dye/Jack Nicklaus creation features some of the most memorable par 3s in golf and influenced golf course design for several generations.

1970—Blind champion Charlie Boswell aced the 141-yard fourteenth hole at Vestavia Country Club in Birmingham, Alabama, with a 6 iron.

1971—In a truly out-of-this-world shot, astronaut Alan Shepherd smuggled a 6 iron club head into his spaceship and screwed it to a lunar excavating tool and hit three balls across the surface of the moon.

1972—Tom Doty recorded a mind-boggling 10-under par for four holes at Brookwood, Illinois, Country Club. His binge included a double eagle, two holes in one, and an eagle.

1973—Johnny Miller shocked the golf world by firing a record sixty-three in the final round on the notoriously treacherous greens at Oakmont Country Club to win the U.S. Open.

1975—Tommy Moore of Hagerstown, Maryland, became the youngest person to ever double-eagle a hole when he carded a deuce at the 512-yard fourteenth hole at Pinehurst Number Five. He was thirteen years old and his name may be familiar to trivia buffs: In 1968, at the age of six years, one month, and one week, he was the youngest person to ever ace a hole at the time.

Lee Trevino, Jerry Heard, and Bobby Nichols were struck by lightning at the Western Open.

1977—Al Geiberger electrified the golfing world by shooting a fifty-nine at the Colonial Country Club in the second round of the Memphis Classic to set a new PGA Tour eighteen-hole record.

1980—Warner Brothers released to double bogie reviews the golf classic *Caddyshack,* and cries of "It's in the hole!" and "Noonan!" are on their way to becoming ageless golf punch-lines at courses around the world.

1981—Kathy Whitworth became the first woman to earn $1 million in career prize money. She eventually recorded eighty-eight professional victories, more than any other man or woman. She also became the LPGA all-time hole-in-one leader with eleven.

1982—Chief Petty Officer Kevin W. Murray of Chicago set the distance record for the category when he double-eagled the 647-yard second hole at the Guam Navy Club.

1986—Television crews were on hand to film Arnold Palmer making his second consecutive ace in as many days at the 185-yard third hole at the TPC at Avernel in Potomac, Maryland.

Armless golfer Jim Taylor hit the first of eight aces. Taylor lost both arms in a childhood accident in which he grabbed a 7,000-volt power line while climbing on a roof. He was fitted with artificial arms and hooks for hands. The golf club is strapped in with special rubber bands.

1987—Walter Dietz, a blind golfer, aced the 155-yard seventh hole at Manakiki Golf Club, in Willoughby Hills, Ohio.

1988—Pat Sutton passed away possessing perhaps the greatest "eclectic" score on any course. An eclectic or "ringer" score is when a golfer takes the best he or she's shot on each hole on a particular course over the number times the individual has played it. Sutton was the former head pro at Riverside Golf Club in Portland, Oregon, where he'd aced all four par 3s, double-eagled one par 5 and eagled the others, and eagled every par 4 on the par 72 course. That's a ringer score of 35, or 37-under par.

1989—In one of the most inexplicable events in all of sports, four golfers—Doug Weaver, Mark Wiebe, Jerry Pate, and Nick Price—during a two-hour spree aced the 160-yard sixth hole at the Oak Hill Country Club in Rochester, New York.

1990—Blind golfer Margaret Waldron aced the eighty-seven-yard seventh hole at Long Point Golf Course on Amelia Island, Florida. Incredibly, the seventy-four-year-old accomplished the feat again the very next day on the same hole with the same club and the same lucky ball.

1991—High school senior Larry Alford lost his left arm below the elbow in a car accident. Using a special prosthesis, he continued to golf and carded his first of three competitive aces in 1994 before moving on to a motivational speaking career that included twelve more aces at corporate golf events.

Brittany Andres, age six years and nineteen days, scored an ace at the eighty-five-yard second hole at the Jimmy Clay Golf Club in Austin, Texas.

1992—Rose Montgomery, ninety-six, became the oldest woman to score an ace. It happened at the 100-yard seventh hole at Canyon Country Club in Palm Springs, California, and is the tenth in her career. In addition, she beat her age by four strokes.

Jeff Sluman became the first golfer to ever ace the 213-yard fourth hole at Augusta National during the Masters.

1993—Television microphones at the Ryder Cup at the Belfry in Sutton Coldfield, England, overhear Nick Faldo tell his caddie, "This would be a good time to hole one," seconds before he uses a 6 iron to ace the fourteenth hole on his way to halving a crucial match with Paul Azinger.

1994—Alabama basher Mike Hilyer aced the 356-yard par 4 first hole at the Pines in Millbrook, Alabama. It would be the first of ten aces Hilyer recorded, incredibly, all of them on par 4s. In "My 2000," in the *Golf Journal,* the official publication of the USGA, David Shefter wrote an article substantiating nine of them (the tenth came six months after the article was published).

1996—Shaun Lynch of Devon, England, set the record for the longest hole in one on a dogleg when he aced the 496-yard seventeenth hole at Teign Valley Club in Christow, England.

In what *Golf World* magazine called a "course in one," first-tee jitters caused Neville Rowlandson, fifty-six, to skull his tee shot at the Felixstowe Ferry Golf Club in Suffolk, England. The ball struck a forward tee marker, ricocheted to the right, bounded twenty-five yards and struck the pin on number eighteen, and dropped into the cup. In what is, perhaps, an apocryphal utterance, Rowlandson's caddie was supposed to have said, "Congratulations, you've just set a new course record."

1999—Lee Janzen aced the 145-yard seventeenth hole at the CVS Charity Classic in Barrington, Rhode Island, and won a new car being offered by a local car dealer. Scott McCarron followed it by crowding the cup with an ace all his own. McCarron, however, didn't get a car.

2000—Legendary golf course architect Robert Trent Jones, Sr., died at the age of ninety-three. He once responded to complaints of unfairness about his redesigned fourth hole at Baltusrol Golf Club's Lower Course in Springfield, New Jersey, by acing the hole on the first swing.

2001—Lee Trevino earned the most lucrative ace in history at the ESPN Shootout at Treetops Resort in Gaylord, Michigan. Trevino aced the 138-yard seventh to earn $1,010,000 ($1 million per ace, with $10,000 for being indisputably closest to the pin).

Jake Paine set an unofficial record for youngest ace by knocking in a 66-yard uphill shot at the Lake Forest Golf and Practice Course in Lake Forest, California. Jake was exactly three years, five months, and fifteen days old. In a fine bit of historical irony, it is within months of 101-year-old Harold Stilson's ace, making him the oldest person in golf history to score an ace, breaking a record that had stood sixteen years.

PGA Tour Ace Totals

1970 — 15	1979 — 25	1988 — 22	1997 — 31
1971 — 10	1980 — 20	1989 — 32	1998 — 27
1972 — 24	1981 — 17	1990 — 34	1999 — 27
1973 — 26	1982 — 25	1991 — 29	2000 — 31
1974 — 17	1983 — 21	1992 — 33	2001 — 27
1975 — 17	1984 — 22	1993 — 25	2002 — 40
1976 — 16	1985 — 35	1994 — 44	
1977 — 16	1986 — 21	1995 — 35	
1978 — 33	1987 — 30	1996 — 39	

Prior to 1970, the PGA Tour did not keep records on cumulative holes in one. Unlike the LPGA, it still does not account for individual aces. The numbers are fairly interesting in that there is no logical pattern to the totals. The low came in 1971, during the still ripe heydays of legends Jack Nicklaus, Arnold Palmer, Tom Weiskopf, and Lee Trevino, each of whom won Tour events that year. The four majors, in order, were won by Charles Coody, Trevino, Trevino, and Nicklaus. Could it be that, like the Tour itself, none of these men cared much about aces? That's hard to believe.

The high of forty-four comes in pre-Tiger 1994, an era when ratings and interest were down and golf was wondering when a golden boy would arrive to energize the sport. The majors were won that year, again in order, by Jose Maria Olazabal, Ernie Els, Nick Price, and, again, Nick Price. Other '94 winners include Fred Couples, Mike Springer, and Tom Lehman, a solid group, but certainly more workmanlike than those of the ace-impoverished years in the early 1970s.

Six of the years in the 1970s had ace totals in the mid-teens, but then in 1978 (major winners, Gary Player, Andy North, Jack Nicklaus, and John Mahaffey) the ace totals more than double from thirty-three after going seventeen in 1974 and 1975, and sixteen in 1976 and 1977.

What happened in those years of bumper crop aces? Did the pros get better? Did the courses get easier? No, many of the same golfers were swinging the same types of clubs at balls that did not get smaller and aiming them at holes that did not all of a sudden get bigger.

The only conclusion left for any analytical thinker is . . .

When it comes to aces, you just never know.

Thanks to Sal Johnson of *Golf* magazine for compiling the following individual ace stats, published November 2002.

Note: Trying to discern the exact number any pro has had is a tricky business. These are the ones made during PGA Tour events. When asked for their individual totals most pros only count the ones made on Tour or during matches.

Most Holes in One on the PGA Tour Since 1970

Hal Sutton	9	Lanny Wadkins	7	Larry Rinker	6
Bob Tway	7	Gibby Gilbert	6	Loren Roberts	6
Hubert Green	7	Gil Morgan	6	Scott Hoch	6

Other Top Players Since 1970

Johnny Miller	5	Nick Price	3	Ernie Els	2
Tom Watson	4	Curtis Strange	3	Fred Couples	1
Phil Mickelson	4	Tom Kite	2	Davis Love III	1
Tiger Woods	3	Greg Norman	2	David Duval	0

Most do not count those made during exhibitions or practice rounds.

Political Aces

BY THE VERY NATURE of their chosen professions, no one should consider any politician "lucky." From the lowliest school board member to the occupant of the highest office in the land, their most well-reasoned decisions and best-intentioned votes usually wind up infuriating at least 49 percent of the people to whom they're obliged to suck up or risk losing their votes.

If they are lucky and, again, they aren't at all lucky, they get elected to higher and more prestigious offices in which they're forced to suck up to special interests or risk losing elections and get busted back down to county road supervisor. They spend long, lonely evenings trapped in airports awaiting flights to distant outposts to explain their position on farm bills. When someone finally breaks the tedium by recognizing them from the Sunday morning news shows they demand to know why they're either for or against a no-win controversial issue—and spend the next forty-five minutes trying to change their minds.

For the honest politician, it's a tiring, thankless job. For the dishonest ones, sure, there are a lot of posh perks, but you're always running the risk of getting busted in a sting operation or, worse, developing a conscience.

So you can't call them lucky but, hey, they're the ones who left cushy desk jobs in the private sector to run for office so it's perfectly fair to call them stupid. But as we've already learned, hole-in-one luck can be bestowed on the blind, the drunk, the feeble, and the hopelessly inexperienced. There's no reason politicians should be excluded.

Presidential Golf History

An unlikely triumvirate of worldly, powerful men sat in plush chairs in smoke-filled rooms with weighty matters on their mind. It was the late 1910s and the world was a tumultuous place. A virulent influenza outbreak had killed an estimated 20 million around the world, Communist and fascist rumblings were beginning to stir in Europe in the wake of the War to End All Wars, and here in America the suffragette movement meant that in a few scant years—yikes!—women would have the right to vote.

Clearly, there was only one course of bold action for the old, white men who made the decisions that decide our daily fates.

Time for golf!

Herbert Hoover, Calvin Coolidge, and William H. Taft, men who at one time or another would reside in the White House and lead the United States as its president, were among the first chief executives in the country to be bitten by the golf bug. They were three of the elite behind the founding of Congressional Country Club in Bethesda, Maryland, a club that for more than eighty years has hosted countless politicians who escape nearby Washington for a round of golf at one of America's most prominent golf courses. It is here that every golfing president since 1924, at one time or another, has teed it up under the watchful eye of Secret Service agents.

The club opened with President and Mrs. Calvin Coolidge presiding; the new club's first president was future Chief Executive Herbert Hoover. Both men were "Founding Life Members," as were William Howard Taft, Woodrow Wilson, and Warren G. Harding, all past U.S. presidents. Other prominent figures who helped launch Congressional were a who's who of entertainment and industry leaders including Charlie Chaplin and John D. Rockefeller, and names such as Astor, Carnegie, DuPont, and Pillsbury.

Golfing at the venerable Blue Course, a Robert Trent Jones, Sr., redesign and the host of multiple majors, is a cherished perk of high office—senators, congressmen and women, ambassadors, heads of state. Ah, if the paneled walls of the Congressional locker rooms could speak, they'd probably say, "What a bunch of losers!"

Political aces are such a rarity that each has been exhaustively documented and it's unlikely that a politician who'd aced would refrain from calling a prime-time press conference to announce the news.

"No politicians of note have ever had an ace at Congressional," says head pro Brad Myers. "You'd think after all these years and all these rounds some of them would have had a hole in one, but there are none. None of the founders—Coolidge, Hoover, or Taft—had ever done it."

Myers says there have been a number of fine golfers from the halls of Congress who were members at Congressional and none of them has ever aced. Congressional Country Club, which you'd figure to be a treasure chest of ace stories is, often like the public coffers to which the politicians are entrusted to oversee, empty.

William Howard Taft (1909–13)

Never had an ace and it probably saved his life—or the life of some hapless caddie. The rotund 355-pound Cincinnati native was the largest man to ever occupy the Oval Office and was larger than many presidential running mates tossed together in a big sack. He needed his caddie to put the ball on the tee for him. Many hole-in-one shooters report a surge of adrenaline that might not have been healthful for a man the bulk of Taft, and if he was so overcome with enthusiasm about his fortune and started jumping up and down, well, watch out.

Theodore Roosevelt, known for his robust nature, urged Taft to give up the game for fear that people would resent him for being involved in a such a rich man's sport and would take it out on him at the polls. He ignored the advice and lost the election of 1912 to a rich man who made no secret of his golfing addiction.

Woodrow Wilson (1913–21)

Diplomat, statesman, philosophic golfer, Wilson was known to play six rounds a week in all kinds of weather. In winter, he'd golf with red balls so he could see them in the snow. His caddies were required to carry flashlights for night golf and he once played a match that didn't end until 5 A.M. He considered the game a delightful pastime and didn't care for its competitive elements so he never kept score. He once said: "Golf is an ineffectual attempt to put an illusive ball into an obscure hole with implements ill-suited to the purpose."

Calvin Coolidge (1923–29)

There is probably a very good reason why the thirtieth president never had an ace. "Silent Cal's" 1925 inaugural address included the telling line "Economy is idealism in its most practical form." The man was especially economical when it came to golf balls. It was said he purposely hit only short shots so he wouldn't risk losing one. Good thing the man died nearly seventy years before the introduction of the pricey Pro V1s.

One of golf's oldest truisms can be applied to Coolidge and why he never aced.

Never up, never in.

Franklin Delano Roosevelt (1933–45)

An avid golfer before being stricken with polio and rendered wheelchair-bound in 1921. Never had an ace. Still, he did have some exploits that would have earned him bonus points in Ron Garland's "Golf Nuts Society." FDR played a round of golf at St. Andrews—on his honeymoon!

General Dwight D. Eisenhower (1953–61)

One of the most avid golfers to ever hold the office of president, it was said he'd golfed 800 times while president. A legendary war hero, he came along at a time when Arnold Palmer began his ascent to legendary status and the two became close friends. According to the Eisenhower Presidential Library in Abilene, Kansas, he aced the 104-yard par 3 at Seven Lakes Country Club in Palm Springs, California, in 1968, seven years after he'd left office.

John F. Kennedy (1961–63)

This gifted golfer might be the only one on earth who actually was horrified at the thought of acing at the beguiling Cypress Point Golf Club on the Eden-like Monterey Peninsula in California. Kennedy was in the midst of a heated race with Richard M. Nixon to succeed President Eisenhower. Kennedy feared that if he scored a hole in one, news reports would race around the country that "another golfer was trying to get in the White House." He never got an ace, but won the election over another golfer, who, within a year, would get a consolation ace that he said was better than a landslide victory.

Richard M. Nixon (1969–74)

Socially maladroit, you wouldn't think he'd be the kind of man who would take to golf. As a child, his cousin, author Jessamyn West, said of Nixon, "He wasn't a little boy that you wanted to pick up and hug." If that's the case, then there were some awkward embraces at the Bel Air Country Club on September 4, 1961. An 18-handicapper, the then-forty-eight-year-old Nixon used a Spalding 5 iron to knock his Spalding ball 144 yards into the second hole at the Bel Air Country Club in Los Angeles. He later called it, "the greatest thrill of my life—even better than being elected." The ace came during a fine round when Nixon, an 18-handicapper, carded an 81. Still, it being Nixon, every silver lining came with a dark cloud: The day cost him three bucks.

During the dark Watergate years, Nixon said golf "became my lifesaver" because it offered exercise and the companionship of close friends.

Gerald R. Ford (1974–77)

Bob Hope got reams of material from Gerald R. Ford's propensity for hitting spectators with errant tee shots. But the man deserves his due. He was the first former president to be a regular golfer at pro-am tournaments where spectators strained the gallery ropes to watch the mighty whack away. If one or two of them got knocked on the noggin in the process, well, that's bound to happen. But Ford had the chops for big-time golf. He was on the University of Michigan football team from 1931 to 1934 and earned tryouts with both the Green Bay Packers and the Detroit Lions. Peter Landau, a coauthor with Shep Campbell of *Presidential Lies: The Illustrated History of White House Golf* (Hungry Minds Publishing, 1998), says Ford was the second-best presidential golfer behind Kennedy.

Many voters resented his pardon of Watergate conniver Richard Nixon, and Ford, America's only unelected president, was drummed out of office by Jimmy Carter, a non-golfing peanut farmer. Still, the loss allowed Ford to golf and just six months after leaving office he had a memorable ace at the Danny Thomas Memphis Classic at the Colonial Country Club's 157-yard fifth hole. He used a 5 iron.

A plaque commemorating the feat, which was witnessed by playing partner Ben Crenshaw, was dedicated at the site. On the twenty-fifth anniversary of the shot, Ford spoke to organizers of the FedEx St. Jude Classic about what was called, "The Shot Heard 'Round the World."

"It was an unforgettable experience," said the one-time 11-handicapper. "I never anticipated it. So I was overwhelmingly thrilled. I couldn't see it when it went in, but the crowd went ecstatic, and I knew something had happened."

Attempts to learn more about Ford and his ace were rebuffed by Martin J. Allen at the Gerald Ford Museum in Grand Rapids, Michigan. I informed Mr. Allen of my project and said I'd like to learn about the details of his ace.

"I wouldn't tell you even if I knew them," he sniffed.

I replied that I didn't know the former president's golf game was a state secret.

"Hey!" Allen exclaimed, "You don't have to be a smart ass about it."

Actually, his reply left me no option. A polite question about a happy event should not be greeted with hostility. It would be like shouting expletives at some well-meaning soul inquiring about someone's grandchildren.

I eventually wrote Ford's office in Palm Springs, California, and was told he's not doing many interviews these days.

Author's note: It was the second time President Ford or one of his surrogates abruptly took offense at one of my questions. The first came at a joint press conference preceding a current events forum with Presidents Carter and Ford in 1987 at Vanderbilt University. The two had been swapping turns answering questions when I asked a question clearly aimed at Carter, whose turn it was to respond.

"Sir, respectfully, where has the Reagan presidency succeeded where yours failed and does the president ever seek your advice?"

I thought these were great questions for Carter because he had a reputation for forthrightness and it was well known that Reagan wouldn't call Carter if he and Nancy were locked out in the cold and his predecessor was the only one who knew where the spare White House keys were hidden.

I was eagerly awaiting his answer when, out of the blue (not to mention out of turn), Ford thundered at me, "I'll let history be the judge of whether or not my presidency was a failure and President Reagan and his staff regularly call to consult with me on major foreign and domestic issues . . ."

He continued for another minute or so about how buddy-buddy he and Reagan were while I was too dumbstruck to even write down what he was saying. All I remember is feeling somehow invigorated by my first presidential scolding and that Carter was thrilled with the question. His eyes brightened and he looked right at me, eagerly nodding, and holding an index finger up in the air while waiting for Ford to finish. But Ford wouldn't finish. He just kept listing achievement after achievement from one of the briefest and least distinguished presidencies in history.

Finally, the moderator stepped in and said, "Thank you for your questions," and ushered the two toward the wings as Ford gave me one final glare. Carter, however, gave me a friendly smile and an "Oh well!" shrug and was gone.

To this day, I'm steadfast in my belief that when Carter got home that night he told his wife, "Rosalynn, this bright young fellow asked me the best question tonight, but that bigmouthed Ford didn't let me get a word in edgewise."

Still, I bear Ford no ill-will and once purchased a "WIN!" (Whip Inflation Now!) button for a quarter at a yard sale. I remember seeing it at the bottom of a box in the garage a few years ago.

George H. W. Bush (1989–93)

He was not the best golfing president, but he was the fastest. He takes pride in finishing an eighteen-hole round in under three hours, and comes from an illustrious golf family. Still, there is no record that any of the Bush clan has ever had a hole in one.

Bush has played many rounds at Webhannet Golf Club in Kennebunk Beach. It was there that Maine Senator Edmund Muskie, a Democrat, aced the 153-yard eleventh hole, eight months before Muskie and presidential running mate Hubert Humphrey got electorally thumped by Nixon and Spiro Agnew in the election of 1968. If Bush was there that day, there is no record, but maybe he zipped past so quickly he didn't notice the commotion.

Bill Clinton (1993–2001)

Bill Clinton is another avid presidential golfer who's never made a hole in one. Because that previous line too obviously lends itself to predictable cheap jokes, there will be no further discussion.

George W. Bush (2001–)

Another lightning fast golfer who's never enjoyed ace lightning on the course. Best known for delivering a stirring speech to the members of the 1999 U.S. Ryder Cup team on the eve of their incredible comeback victory over European golfers. His brother, Florida Governor Jeb Bush, is reportedly a better golfer, but none of the golfing Bushes has ever scored an ace.

U.S. Supreme Court Justices

The 111 men and 2 women who have made up the U.S. Supreme Court cloak themselves in more than just black robes. They are cloaked in mystery. They do not answer to the press, to the politicians, and certainly not to golf writers who want to know if they can bang a 6 iron with the same sort of authority with which they bang a gavel.

But a friendly spokeswoman, herself cloaked in a bit of nameless anonymity, does.

She said just two of the U.S. Supreme Court Justices who have regally ruled America without fear of electoral trifling have made aces. In fact, the two justices each voted on the controversial PGA Tour, Inc. v. Martin case and came down on the side of the disabled golfer, joining the 7–2 majority in ruling that Martin's use of a cart did not represent an unfair advantage.

Even more interesting is that while it took a president 192 years to appoint a woman to the high court, the first one struck a blow for equality by becoming the second justice to ace. The first was current Justice John Paul Stevens, who, in 1990, apparently aced the lovely Snowmass Club in Aspen, Colorado, although Ken Everett, the pro at the time, does not recall it.

"Gee, back then we made a real big deal out of aces because there weren't too many of them at Snowmass," Everett says. "Maybe he did and just—ho hum—ducked out the back without letting anybody know."

Of course, no one is questioning the justice's integrity. If there's one group of people you wouldn't require swearing on stack of Bibles for truthfulness, it is the justices from the U.S. Supreme Court.

More of a fuss was made when the second Supreme aced.

It was Sandra Day O'Connor and she'd just escaped Washington and the tumultuous Supreme Court decision that ensured fellow golfer George W. Bush would be president instead of then-Vice President Al Gore, a man no one's ever confused for any sort of swinger.

"She has a real aura about her, but she's the humblest person in the world," says Andy Fellows, who was working at the Paradise Valley Country Club near Phoenix, Arizona, the day O'Connor deadlocked the Supreme Court in the male vs. female aces category. "It was a week after that historic vote, in fact, the vote was the reason she'd delayed her trip to Arizona. So it was really something to see her just walking through the clubhouse like a regular person happy to be out golfing in the sunshine."

Course construction had forced the course to use temporary tees on number eight and shorten what had been a par 4 to a 150-yard par 3. Fellows says the shot was straight into the sun and neither O'Connor nor her playing partners saw the ball go in.

"But it was in the hole when they got there," he said. "At the turn she came in and didn't say a word. She was just smiling and pleasant, like always. At the turn her husband and the people she was golfing with came in and told us about her ace. I went out to the tenth tee and started kidding her, 'So how'd that front nine go? Anything unusual happen?' She just smiled and said, 'Yes, it was very exciting. A hole in one!'"

Still, mindful of decorum and her stature in society, Fellows said O'Connor did not guzzle booze, remove articles of clothing, or shout, "I am the greatest!" the way other golfers have been known to do upon getting their first ace.

"No, she's ever refined. A real lady. And a pretty fair golfer. She usually shoots in the 85 to 95 range."

Head pro Duff Lawrence made a traditional plaque for her commemorating the ace and members of Paradise Valley Country Club wonder if, as she's deliberating the weighty affairs of the United States and the laws that will determine how we live for years to come, she doesn't look up at the plaque and the ball and think, however briefly, of topics delightfully different from the rule of law.

Vice President J. Danforth Quayle (1989–93)

Former Vice President Dan Quayle is a firebrand conservative who can be counted on to warm the right while inflaming the left. But when it comes to golf he's so nonpartisan he leans straight up. In fact, his love for the game can even provoke words that could be considered, well, not unkind about the Oval Office liberal the GOP despises the most.

Yep, golf is the détente that brings Quayle and Bill Clinton together.

"There were a lot of conservatives who criticized Bill Clinton for golfing so much while in office," Quayle said in an interview from his Phoenix office. "I did not. In fact, that's probably the only thing he did in office I didn't criticize."

Generously, Quayle even refrained from saying he was happy when Clinton was anywhere but the Oval Office.

Though he won't say so—his money's on Kennedy—Quayle's probably the best golfer to ever run for president. His handicap's been as low as a plus one in college and has never been higher than an 8.

His passion for golf even causes him to break one of the cardinal rules of politics by disagreeing on the record with the man who chose him to be his vice president. He thinks former President George Bush was a kook—not his word—when it comes to his approach to the game.

"I played with him a few times and, to me, it's not enjoyable," Quayle says. "I'm all for fast play, but he wants to get in a round in two and a half hours or less. He just races through it. It's like he starts each day off with a list and if it says, 'Play golf,' he just wants to get through with it so he can cross it off the list and move on to the next thing. That's no way to play golf."

Quayle's had two aces: the first as a senior in high school to win the club championship at La Fontaine Country Club—it made all the local papers; the second was in 1978 on the tenth hole at Pine Valley when he was a thirty-one-year-old U.S. congressman—he fought to keep it out of all the papers.

"Even though it was a weekend and I didn't miss any votes, I didn't want the story about me getting a hole in one to leak to the press. I knew they'd use it against me."

He swears the secrecy wasn't to avoid having to buy a pricey round of drinks at the exclusive club.

"No, but I know the type who would. I remember golfing at a club back home in Indiana and this one guy had a reputation for being a terrible tightwad. He had an ace on the fifteenth hole and as soon as it went in people back at the club were calling friends and telling them to get down there because this so-and-so was going to have to buy. Everyone knew it would kill him to buy drinks. Well, he never did. When he got to the green, he picked his ball out of the cup and walked off the course. Just went straight to the parking lot. What a tightwad!"

The aces and his skillful golfing history make him take umbrage with quotes from two famous Americans: Richard Nixon and Will Rogers. Nixon said that his hole in one was "the greatest thrill of (his) life, better even than being elected."

"Getting an ace is very exciting, but it's a lot of luck. Winning an election is much more rewarding."

And for Will Rogers, who noted that rail splitting produced a great president in Abraham Lincoln, but that golf, for all its millions of devoted participants, "hasn't produced even an 'A-number one' congressman," Quayle says he's proud of his contributions. In fairness to Quayle and other golfing politicians, Rogers made the comment during the Great Depression when Republican Herbert Hoover was running the country into the ground.

Quayle was such a good sport, it was not even uncomfortable asking him about another famous quote, this one made by his wife, Marilyn, when the press was reporting salacious rumors that he may have been unfaithful to her during a golf vacation.

She said, "Anyone who knows Dan knows he's much more interested in golfing than sex."

"Hey! That's her quote," he says, laughing. "I don't care to talk about it, other than to say she was mad at me when she said it."

And he said no more, not even when given an opportunity to come out in favor of one over the other. But that's a politician for you. When there are two powerful special interest groups involved, in this case golf lovers and lovers of sex, a smart politician's always going to straddle the fence.

It's in the Stars: Celebrity Aces

THEIR BREATHTAKING GOOD LOOKS grace the pages of glossy $5.00 magazines eager to trumpet their wisdoms, their fancy baubles, and their supermodel date mates. They get paid millions of dollars to make movies we stand in line to see. We buy their books, their endorsed products, and tune in in droves to watch them weep with Barbara Walters.

Yes, it's a charmed life being a celebrity. Everyone fawns over you to ensure your every wish is granted. If—and it better not be you—some minimum-wage slob slops some soup on their $2,000 Italian suit, that working person could be fired and sent home to deal with the shame of soiling some celebrity duds. The meal, of course, will be provided gratis, but wasn't that the deal anyway?

There is no more regal existence in America than to be a smiling celebrity. Have one hit movie or TV show, sing a catchy pop ditty, or hit a game-winning home run and everywhere you go your magnificent presence will ensure that magical things happen. Most of them to you.

Everywhere except the golf course.

For if America were more like golf, there would be no prejudice, no tax hula hoops for shifty CEOs who need them least, and no magic carpet rides through our daily lives that challenge and frustrate the rest of us.

Happily, celebrity luck doesn't seem to translate to golf luck. Sure, they get to play better courses than you and I—often for free—but the game frustrates them every bit as much as it does us on a $29 weekend round at the local muni. When it comes to aces, golf is just as stingy with celebrities as it is with the rest of us. It plays no favorites and seeks no autographs in return for a lucky bounce.

> **LUCKY SIGN**
> *In Brazil, members of certain tribes wear freeze-dried piranha—a deadly fish—on pendants around their necks.*

The Celebrity Teacher

Fine-print screen credits are lousy with the names of otherwise anonymous people who are responsible for the choreography, dialogue, and appearance of every top actor and actress in a multimillion-dollar Hollywood production. If those hired minions fail, they can be replaced within an hour by similar "coaches" who will correct their shortcomings. And then if those people fail, the actors and actresses themselves can be entrusted to handle the matters themselves because, after all, what are choreography, dialogue, and appearance but walking, talking, and dressing ourselves, elementary skills we can reasonably expect from even our dimmest preschoolers. Those names get screen credit, but the one name you may never see down in the fine print when most of us have left the theater to complain about the stupid movie is the name of the coach who means more to most celebrities than even top producers who pay their gaudy salaries: Ron del Barrio.

He is the former head pro at Studio City Golf Course near Hollywood (see, stars are so coddled they get a golf course at their place of work, something to think about the next time your union says it will go to the mat over a better dental plan). These days he's doing a little bit of teaching and is in numerous entertainment business ventures with his good friend rocker Eddie Van Halen.

Del Barrio cowrote a wonderful series of stories about being golf pro to the stars for the now-defunct *Maximum Golf* magazine. In it, he related stories about how Jack Nicholson is so single-minded on the golf course he will drive first and then stroll down the fairway while his befuddled partners quietly argue about whether they should just walk after him or risk his volcanic fury by hitting their drives over his head; he revealed how Tommy Lee kept him up on an all-night booze binge and then dragged him to his personal tattoo artist (something no one should be without) to have the inkster engrave a rose on his arm; and how Sylvester Stallone took good-natured offense at his Rocky impersonation of the star and punched him so hard in the arm he swears it knocked the petals off the rose.

He drops names the way Tiger drops three-foot birdie putts—not to show off, but just because that's the way he earns his living. Here are his takes on some top celebrity golfers, only one of whom has carded an ace. Can you guess which one? The answer follows.

Joe Pesci

"As awkward as his swing looks, he's a killer when there is money on the table. Absolutely nothing rattles him. If there are big bucks on the line and he needs to make a par, birdie—whatever—you do not want to bet against him."

Will Smith

"He's serious about golf and he's good at it. Most golfers want to stand at the range and just bomb away with the driver, but that's not how you get good. Will understands that you practice the game from the cup out, not the other way around. He practices to get good with his putts and chips and then his irons, and he knows that way the rest of the game will fall right into place. He laid out $250,000 to join Sherwood Country Club and then built a par-3 hole in his backyard with two different tees so he can hit balls from 105- and 150-yards. That's a man who knows his golfing priorities. If he wasn't so in demand right now, he'd be a really fine golfer."

David Leisure

"Most people know this guy as Joe Isuzu, but he's a tremendous golfing talent who plays to a 2 handicap. He has a phenomenal short game and really knows how to work the ball around a course to his benefit. He's at a level where he can fade or draw a ball depending on the shot he needs. A really talented golfer, and that's no lie."

Tommy Lee

"He is one lucky, er, let's say he's one lucky guy on the golf course. I've never seen anyone get the lucky golf bounces the way he does. He'll hit a ball so awful and it'll bounce off a tree, hit a rake, and roll right up on the green. He'll be smiling and laughing and saying, 'Did you see that! What a great shot! That's the greatest shot in the world!' I'll say, 'Uh, Tommy, you shanked that ball. It was heading right at that Mercedes in the parking lot. You were lucky it hit that tree.' And he'll say, 'Yeah, but what a great shot! Let's go get some Jagermeister!' Great shot or bad shot, he's always leaving the course to go get some more Jagermeister. The guy's a full-time party."

Jon Lovitz

"Let's say as a golfer he makes a really fine tennis player. He's really thrilled when he hits the green. One time I was playing with Jack Nicholson and we came up on Jon, Dana Carvey, and the late, great Phil Hartman. Dana starts doing his Jack Nicholson. Jack laughs and we're all having fun. We play through—Jack plays through everybody—and he says, 'Nice guys . . . who the hell were they?' I'm surprised he doesn't recognize them and say, 'Jack, that was Phil Hartman, Dana Carvey, and Jon Lovitz from *Saturday Night Live*. Three of the funniest guys on the planet. Don't you ever watch the show?' He says to me, 'I watch it every @#$*# week. Wouldn't miss it for the world.' That's Jack."

Sylvester Stallone

"Forget everything you think you know about Sylvester Stallone. He became famous playing Rocky and Rambo, guys not known for their thoughtfulness, but of all my celebrity clients, he's got the best potential to get his handicap down to scratch. He has no ego and understands that golf is like chess, you have to be thinking two or three shots ahead. He does that. He's a real thinker on the course and a student of the game. He has a phenomenal swing and is my best student. Very cerebral. I saw him shoot a 76 at a very difficult Wood Ranch Golf Club in Simi Valley, California. A truly great golfer who wants to get even better."

Denzel Washington

"A very gifted athlete with a great understanding of the game. He's my favorite type of student because he always shows up with a wedge. He's only been playing the game for a few years, but he knows you need to learn the short game if you're ever going to get better. His problem is that he's such a great actor, they're all paying him big money for big roles. The guy doesn't have any time to get better at golf."

Richard Dreyfuss

"As a golfer, Richard Dreyfuss makes one helluva actor. Let's leave it at that."

Jack Nicholson

"Everyone who reads the papers knows Jack can really swing a club. Everyone remembers that traffic incident a few years ago when he pulled out a 5 iron and smashed some guy's windshield. He probably didn't think he was doing anything wrong because it's Jack's world and we're all just living in it. He just loves to golf and is a 12-handicapper. There are times when I wouldn't want to play with him and I don't think I'd ever want to play in front of him. He doesn't wait for anyone else to hit and just hits into everybody anywhere on the golf course. He's not doing it to be rude, but when Jack's ready to hit, he hits. It's up to the rest of us to get the hell out of the way."

Jack Wagner

"This guy has Tour-level golf talent. A really great golfer. And he's special in that he plays better when the stakes are higher. Don't bet with Jack—unless you have a few thousand dollars you don't mind losing."

Richard Roundtree

"He loves golf so much that I don't call him Shaft anymore. I call him Graphite Shaft."

Kevin Costner

"He doesn't hit it real far, but he works hard on his swing. Absolutely loves the game and the time he spends on the course."

Arnold Schwarzenegger

"He's very athletic and knows you cannot buy a swing—something few of his trend-chasing colleagues understand. They think golf's cool and they want to play, but they aren't willing to invest the time it takes to learn the game. Everything else comes easy to them and they think golf should, too. That's not the way it works and Arnold understands that. Arnold's taller and thicker than Stallone, even, but he knows golf is a finesse game. He can hit the ball a ton, but he's never swung more than 70 percent. That's great control. He can get so annoyed that he'll chew his cigar down to a stub. Golf can really torment the old testosterone in an action star."

Answer: Sylvester Stallone. Del Barrio, Stallone, and Jack Nicholson were playing the par 3 layout at Studio City when Stallone aced a 110-yard hole with an easy wedge.

"The ball landed ten feet past the hole, but just sucked

right back in for the ace," del Barrio says. "Jack can't believe it. He gets this look on his face and says, 'Jesus, what a great shot! Did you see that #@!*&# thing back up? That's just great!' Stallone just looks at me and winks and says, 'Hey, thank you, thank you.' I don't think he wanted Jack to see, but he was thrilled. I was with him one time when he had a great eagle on a par 5 and he let it out then. The putt dropped and he said, 'Bring on Apollo Creed. I'll kick his ass!' He loves the game.

"Still, if you're looking for a really great time, just hope you're in the foursome or anywhere on the course the day Tommy Lee gets an ace. Man, that's going to be some party."

⌐ ⬤

Athletic Aces

Don Zimmer

Picturing bug-eyed Yankee bench coach Don Zimmer outside a dugout—much less on a plush tee box golfing like he's a scratch sharpshooter—seems as farfetched as brain surgeons operating with catcher's mitts.

But there was Zimmer on February 23, 2001, his 9 iron high above his head as he and Yankee greats Rich Gossage, Mel Stottlemyre, and Ron Guidry watched his tee shot sail through the skies above the 125-yard twelfth hole at Wentworth Golf Club in Tarpon Springs, Florida.

The foursome had been participants and witnesses to historic feats on the baseball diamond, but that day they saw something truly remarkable.

Zimmer aced. His first. He waved off advice to stash the ball for safekeeping: "No way! This ball's bringing me luck!"

He dubbed his very next shot straight into a pond on his way to scoring a 135.

John Elway

Future Hall of Famer John Elway is a staple of the Celebrity Golf Tour and a 4-handicapper. A two-time Super Bowl champion, he's been a catalyst in some of football's most memorable games. He was asked during the 2000 Mario Lemieux Celebrity Invitational Open in Pittsburgh what he enjoys about golf.

"I enjoy playing with the guys and smacking the ball around."

What about the thrills of the game?

"Thrills? Are you kidding me? There's no thrill I could get on a golf course that would ever match the thrills I've had on the football field. No way . . . Well, maybe a hole in one. Yeah, that would be a thrill."

One month later on June 28 at the Innisbrook Resort's Island Course in Palm Harbor, Florida, Elway aced with a 3 iron on the 193-yard thirteenth.

In a flourish typical of his gridiron glories, it was Elway's fortieth birthday.

Elway later told reporters: "It's my highlight in golf. I hit a good 3 iron high at the hole. I didn't see it go in. I looked around and went to the hole—there it was. I had a hard time believing it. It's my first ace and to have it happen on my birthday is special."

Carlton Fisk

His home run in the 1975 World Series is considered one of the great moments in baseball, and every fan remembers or has seen replays with Fisk exhorting the ball to stay fair. It is a transcendent and enduringly joyful moment. The home run and a tremendous career earned Fisk a pass into the hallowed Baseball Hall of Fame.

He must have used a similar sort of body English to get his first ace, but that remarkable feat resulted in a considerably less joyful result. Here is what happened, as Fisk told it to Jeff Idelson, one of the many friendly and helpful people at the historic baseball shrine in Cooperstown, New York.

"I was playing in a tournament in Las Vegas about five years ago and Howard Twitty was one of the players in our foursome. I asked him if he'd ever had any holes in one and he said, 'Oh, sure, about ten or so.' Well, Lexus was sponsoring a hole in one on a par 3 and would you believe I had my first hole in one? I won an ES300. Boy, was I excited.

"Well, the IRS was right there to take about $14,000 in taxes. My bar bill for getting the ace was $580. Then it cost me about $1,200 to ship it home to Illinois. On top of that, I was too big to fit in the car so I had to trade up to something I could squeeze into. That cost another $10,000. So my first lucky ace cost me something like $26,000 for a car I didn't need.

"One month later, I am playing in Ron Kittle's tournament and Mercedes is sponsoring a hole in one. Guess what? I whack my ball over the flag, it spins back, hits the stick! Luckily, it rolled about four feet away. I was worried that if I'd have won a Lexus and a Mercedes on holes in one within a month I might have had to have gone back to work."

George Brett

Idelson also relates that Hall of Famer George Brett of the Kansas City Royals had two holes in one within a one-month span, but unlike Fisk, Brett was lucky. He didn't win a thing.

Joe DiMaggio

In 1966, DiMaggio hosted a tournament at the Sharp Park Golf Course in Pacifica, California, and donated a color TV set as a hole-in-one prize at the tournament.

The only ace that day came on the 140-yard fifteenth hole when some lucky guy with an 8 iron hit one in. It was DiMaggio. No word on whether he took the TV he donated.

Rick Rhoden

Some of the best pitchers in baseball are avid golfers. The list includes Atlanta Braves Greg Maddux and John Smoltz, Arizona Diamondbacks Randy Johnson and Curt Schilling, and Mets ace Tom Glavine.

But back before he stopped firing managers and started leaving Joe Torre alone, New York Yankee owner, George Steinbrenner, used to forbid his pitching staff to play golf. He thought it would ruin their batting swings.

"Funny thing was," says former Yankee pitcher Rick Rhoden, "the American League had the designated hitter and a pitcher for the Yankees could go an entire career without having to pick up a bat. Sometimes George just didn't make a lot of sense."

Of course, nobody would pay much attention to such fool-

ACE ART
Sports artist Bob Novack offers hand-numbered and signed by the artist "Good Sports Art Hole in One" lithographs for $124.99. The painting depicts a ball about to drop into a cup just a few inches from a ball mark on the plush green. Far off in the background, a foursome of golfers prepares to celebrate.

---

ishness, especially Rhoden, a scratch golfer and a standout on the Celebrity Golf Tour, who's earned more than $1.5 million since joining the Tour in 1990.

He's had six career aces and says the best tip he's ever had was to play one hole at a time.

You can bet he didn't hear it from Steinbrenner.

Celebrity Aces

The luck of some celebrities does transfer to the golf course. Here is a partial list of some of the Hollywood and entertainment icons who've experienced an ace.

Gummo Marx

The only one of the five fabled Marx Brothers who could possibly be called low-key. He aced the 155-yard second hole at the Tamarisk Country Club in Palm Springs on May 15, 1960. The shot was witnessed by his brothers Harpo and Zeppo and it's possible to imagine the ensuing commotion caused overflying airplanes bound for Los Angeles to seek clearance to land somewhere else. Like Utah.

Bob Hope

He's had six and he deserves every one of them. This is a man who's spent seven decades entertaining American troops overseas in war and civilians at home in peace. He and traveling road partner Bing Crosby (he had an ace, too) helped spread the joy of golf for the masses by hosting wildly popular pro-am tournaments that combined the greatest golfers of their day with stars willing to show they can duff just like the rest of us. His Bob Hope/Chrysler Desert Classic has raised more than $35 million for the Eisenhower Medical Center and other local charities.

The PGA issued him an award for being "one of the three men who've done the most for golf," and he's been enshrined in the World Golf Hall of Fame with a plaque that reads, "Bob Hope—known by all for his nose, applauded for his humor, envied for his wit, and loved by millions for his unselfish concern for all beings, Bob Hope is truly one of a kind. He popularized golf to the unknowing, sponsored it for charity, and played it for fun. Not a golf champion, but a great champion of golf."

His autobiography is called, *Confessions of a Hooker,* and he has repeatedly been quoted as saying, "Golf is my profession. I tell jokes to pay my green fees."

CROONER QUIZ

Q: Which one of these four diverse singers has never had an ace: Alice Cooper, Vic Damone, Perry Como, or Céline Dion?

A: Her most famous song is connected with a really big boat sinking, but one of her tee shots never has. Céline, an avid golfer, may go on forever in search of a hole in one.

Mickey Gilley

It's been said that before Mickey Gilley, the only people who wore cowboy hats were cowboys. But that changed with Gilley and *Urban Cowboy,* the 1980 box office smash starring John Travolta, based on Gilley's, the singer's legendary Pasadena, Texas, honky-tonk.

The success allowed him to be one of the people he used to make fun of when he was a nineteen-year-old kid driving a truck around Houston.

"I'd see these guys golfing at these fancy country clubs and think, 'Man, that's the stupidest thing I've ever seen.'"

His first cousin, Jerry Lee Lewis, helped change that perception. He took him golfing and showed him which end of the tee the ball goes on. Gilley didn't know. But he learned.

"I never dreamed I'd get so caught up in the sport and that one day it would bring me one of the greatest joys of my life," Gilley says.

This is a man who's had seventeen number-one hits, was invited to perform for President Ronald Reagan in the White House, and earned a star on the Hollywood Walk of Fame. What in golf measures up to all that?

"My two holes in one," Gilley says from his Branson, Missouri, theater, where the scorecard is in the dressing room where he can see it before each of his 200 yearly performances. "My adopted son, Danny Wagner, was always bragging about his. I said, "Well, I've had an eagle on a par 4. What's the difference?'

"He said, 'Did you get to write a 1 on your scorecard?' And he got me there. And it is such a difference. It's one of the great thrills of my life."

Clint Eastwood

It didn't make the papers, and that's a pity because the headline writers would have had a ball.

DO YOU FEEL LUCKY? EASTWOOD SURE DOES

Or, HOLE IN ONE MAKES EASTWOOD'S DAY

One of America's greatest icons, an avid golfer for more than fifty years, Eastwood finally got a hole in one at the lovely Carmel Valley Ranch course near his Carmel-by-the-Sea home.

In a Robert Sullivan article for *T&L Golf,* the steely-eyed star of so many classic movies talked about it over a round at his luxurious new club called Tehama.

Eastwood said: "That was a real one. I had one before on a short course, but that was the first real one of my life. It was over at Carmel Valley Ranch [the seventh hole]."

During an interview with *60 Minutes*'s Steve Kroft, Eastwood extemporaneously composed a fine golf analogy for his life, one that many of us should be so lucky as to emulate. He told Kroft that he was on the back nine of his life and was playing a lot better, maybe under par down the home stretch, after a rugged front nine with a lot of triple bogies.

It's good to know, too, that an ace would mean something to someone like Eastwood, someone who has a life that many of us perceive as perfect. He took pains to point out that the ace happened on a "real" hole, a nifty little 110-yarder nestled along the precociously babbling Carmel River. And it's good to know, too, as Sullivan's article points out, Eastwood would have paid homage to one of golf's greatest, if oddest, traditions. He was going to set up the bar, but the luck was still with him.

"We played late," Eastwood said, "and the bar was empty so I didn't have to buy."

Some guys have all the luck.

Best Places for Aces

LET'S FACE IT: Not all golf courses are created equal. If they were, the lines to play Crabgrass Acres for twenty-five bucks would be as long and enthusiastic as they are at storied places like Augusta National, Pebble Beach, TPC at Sawgrass, and Muirfield Village, where a round would cost twenty times that much—and that doesn't include tips for the sexy quench wench on the drink cart. For any golfer, the mere mention of those last four names produces mingled sighs of affection, envy, and lust. Years of loving television coverage has built an affection; we envy those, pro and amateur alike, who get to play there; and we lust after the opportunity to plunge our tees deep into their fertile soils.

(See, even typing their names can turn hack reporters into budding romance novelists.)

If you've never had an ace, you certainly don't care about where it finally happens and any ace at the most downtrodden municipal golf course is an event to be treasured forever. But deep in his or her soul, every golfer from around the world dreams of one day standing on the seventh at Pebble Beach, staring out at the Pacific, and hearing its waves crash like cymbals in a patriotic overture. Just once, you'd like to take a shot at it and the other most famous postcard par 3s in golf. Just to see how you'd do.

What golfer lucky enough to find a genie's lamp on the beach wouldn't use one of the precious wishes for just such an opportunity? But that would only leave you with one wish, and who can choose between world peace and personal riches? Because anyone who wishes to play the great courses would have to burn up the second wish on acing one of their spectacular par 3s.

⌒ ●

Augusta National Golf Club, Augusta, Georgia, 1933

The par 3s here cause more heartbreak than an absentminded flirt. They are stunningly beautiful and tempt you to go ahead, go for it. But at the last second, most golfers find themselves trying to extract their balls from awkward or embarrassing positions.

In the entire history of the Masters, there have been only fourteen made during competition, with probably the most famous story being about a man who is renowned for not hitting any competitive aces.

It happened at the beguiling twelfth hole where infuriatingly fickle winds can slap a ball into Rae's Creek with startling insouciance. It was 1947 and Claude Harmon had the honors.

He proved he'd earned them, too, by being the first player to ever ace the so-called "scariest hole in golf" (only amateur William Hyndman, 1959, and Curtis Strange, 1988, have duplicated the feat). The crowd exploded. The shot brought every man, woman, and child to their feet to shower Harmon with wave upon wave of adulation.

Only one person was nonplussed, the man the Scots called "The Wee Icemon."

It was Ben Hogan. He didn't grunt so much as a charitable "nice shot" in Harmon's direction. He merely waited for the applause to die down so he could put his tee in the ground and hit a shot to within eight feet of the occupied hole.

He kept icily mum during the stroll down the fairway and across the bridge to Rae's Creek. He didn't say anything while Harmon bent to retrieve the lucky ball and graciously acknowledge the still-giddy crowd. Hogan simply lined up his putt and sunk it for birdie.

It wasn't until after both struck their drives on thirteen and were strolling down the fairway that Hogan finally deemed to speak.

"You know back there on the twelfth hole . . ."

"Yes?" Harmon asked expectantly.

"I've been thinking . . . That's the first time I ever birdied that hole."

Shadow Creek Golf Club, Las Vegas, Nevada, 1989

At $37 million, this Tom Fazio/Steve Wynn design is reportedly one of the most expensive golf courses ever made. And because most everyone in America helped build it by going to Vegas and losing money in one of Wynn's casinos, you'd think we'd all get to play there.

Fat chance. It is one of the most exclusive golf courses in the world. You have to either win really, really big or lose really, really, really big to even hope to get invited to play there—and even then, don't be surprised if the $500 green fee shows up on your bill.

For a place so alluringly foreboding, they've picked an oddly inviting man to be assistant head pro. He's Wes Weston and he'll be happy to tell you about his only hole in one. It didn't happen here. In fact, it didn't even happen on a regulation golf course. It happened at a Los Angeles driving range. That might not sound like much, but it sure was special to the thirty-nine-year-old Weston.

"I was so excited I made everyone stop hitting balls and I ran 185 yards out onto the range so I could get the ball out of the hole," he says. "Then I just went back to whacking balls."

Pretty soon, he noticed a familiar figure over his left shoulder. It was a swing he'd seen before.

"Man, there is something about this guy that looks familiar," he thought. It was a foggy, rainy night. Weston looked more closely and finally made the connection. It was a man named Rodney Hamilton, a local golf legend and the man who'd given Weston his very first clubs, a simple gesture that changed a life for good. For good, and for the better.

"To see him there and have him watch me hit that shot, it's something I'll never forget."

Weston was not a pampered child of the posh country clubs, as his position at Shadow Creek would lead one to infer. No, he was born and raised by loving parents in what he calls a "tough, challenging environment."

Many others would describe it as a hopeless, dream-squashing ghetto. It was South Central Los Angeles. Many of his childhood friends are either dead or in jail.

Few of us will ever get to play Shadow Creek or even see the holes those fortunate enough to golf there describe as a wonderland. They are high-rollers, men and women who consider themselves lucky winners.

None of them are as lucky as the winner who still likes to brag about the lonely ace he got on a rainy range back in Los Angeles.

⌣ ⬤

Carmel Valley Ranch, Carmel, California

Clint Eastwood aced the seventh hole here and, sure, that's great, but Clint being Clint, you'd figure he'd have probably aced the spectacular thirteenth hole on this often overlooked gem on the Monterey Peninsula. Buck for buck, it might be the best value course in the country.

And the origin of that value is none other than—surprise, surprise—famed architect Pete Dye, the man whose diabolically lovely layouts have led more than one golfer to speculate about satanic affiliations. But at the Carmel Valley Ranch, Dye's considered something of a saint. He transformed a somewhat routine layout into something sensational.

His fee?

One dollar.

"He designed the course in 1981 and always felt he didn't do it right," says resort spokesman Tom Blackman. "When they asked him to redesign it in 1994, he presented two bills: one for materials and labor and one for his fee. The second bill was for $1.00. He'd said this was some of the most spectacular landscape he'd ever had to work with and he always felt he hadn't done it justice the first time."

Holes ten through fourteen look down across the sun-kissed paradise author John Steinbeck called the "Pastures of Heaven." The thirteenth is a gorgeous scene stealer that dares even the most focused golfers to keep their heads down.

The views and golf challenges are so breathtaking that

even the most frustrated duffer would have to admit: For a buck, the Dye guy did a helluva job.

Riviera Country Club, Los Angeles, 1926
Many golfers never get an ace for the simple reason they never aim at the hole. Sound stupid? How many times have you heard golfers express satisfaction at simply making a shot on the green on a 150-yard par 3? Most golfers have it in them to do better. Need proof? Consider the famous 175-yard sixth hole at the Riviera.

It's called the Donut Hole because it has a big sand trap right in the center of the green. Just like a, mmmmm, dough-nut. You'd think the hole with its narrow circular green would be ace stingy, but you'd be wrong.

Club pro Todd Yoshitake says the hole is generous with the ace, and it's a thrilling result for golfers who feel they've achieved a truly skillful stroke.

"People tend to aim right at the center of the green on every par 3," Yoshitake says. "But at the Donut Hole, there's that great big bunker waiting to devour balls right there. It forces them to aim and execute a better shot."

Olde Stonewall, Ellwood City, Pennsylvania, 1999
Golf Digest called this the number-one public course in Pennsylvania. Pennsylvania? Judging from the enormous two- to twelve-pound limestone boulders that line many of the fairways and approaches, you'd think you'd arrived in ancient Egypt before the work crews put up the pyramids. The back

nine features tremendous elevation changes and two lovely par 3s back to back, the 180-yard fourteenth and the 190-yard fifteenth.

Holes eleven through thirteen wind through the trees and up to the top of a mountain with such dizzying challenges that golfers feel giddy by the time they reach the elevated fourteenth tee built on plateaued terraces of boulder walls. Water cascades over still more boulders to an impetuously swaled green. The fifteenth hole offers a longer, more narrow challenge with a chasm to the left.

No one has ever aced these two back to back. I hope no one ever does.

The sixteenth tee offers a sheer drop of more than 150 feet across another yawning chasm. Anyone coming to that tee after back-to-back aces would have to figure life can't get any better. Dire consequences might ensue.

The Cliffs at Glassy, Glassy Mountain, South Carolina, 1992

The thirteenth tee is on top of a hill, which is on top of a mountain. The effect is not for the faint of heart. With the eastern edge of the Blue Ridge Mountains far in the distance—below your feet—it looks like you're teeing off the wing of a cruising transcontinental jetliner. The green is cuddled by natural rock outcroppings that are capable of pinballing mishit balls into a never-neverland of lost balls. If you're good in this world and get sent to heaven, those who've been blessed to play The Cliffs at Glassy will be heard to say, "Hey, this place looks familiar!"

TPC at Sawgrass, Stadium Course, Ponte Vedra, Florida, 1981

Anyone who doesn't think the golf gods have a malicious sense of humor need look no further than Jim Poole. He's the amiable head pro at the TPC at Sawgrass, home to the most photographed and famous par 3 in golf, the 137-yard seventeenth hole with the island green.

It's the only hole that the PGA Tour deems worthy of covering each and every shot struck to it on its Web site, www.pgatour.com, at the Live@17 link. In just twenty-one years, it has produced a rare kind of mania in all of golf.

"When someone aces number seventeen it is the biggest thrill in their entire golfing lives," Poole says. "I've seen people come into the clubhouse still trembling, literally shaking, because they've just aced seventeen. They say it's an indescribable feeling."

In spring 2002, the seventeenth hole had been aced 112 times by professionals and amateurs since Sawgrass opened, by far the most aces on any hole at the Pete Dye layout, followed by number thirteen with eighty-six; number three with seventy-two, and number eight with sixty-seven.

Not one of those aces was made by Poole, the man responsible for keeping track of them and congratulating the lucky golfer with a commemorative plaque. In fact, he's never had one anywhere.

The man responsible for the course with the most famous par 3 in golf, home to the most sought-after golf ace, has never had one himself. It's his job to play the course and he does so several times each week. Has for years. The odds say he should have aced at least one hole on his home course, especially at the most aced hole, the seventeenth.

It's almost diabolically cruel.

And, yeah, he confesses, it gets to him.

"It doesn't bother me, but I do think about it each and every time I play the course," he says. "Not necessarily on the hole, but at some time or another during each round I think to myself, 'Boy, it sure would be nice to ace seventeenth today.' I think about it all the time."

Think that's cruel? How about this?

Poole tells a story of four members recently playing a twilight round that left them near dark as they came to the island green. The four each hit with ears cocked for telltale signs for it was too dark to see the green.

"They heard two splashes so they knew two balls were in the water," he says. "They get up there and they see one ball on the green. It's a Srixon 2 or whatever. The one guy says, 'Oh, that's mine.' Well, the other guy was playing a Srixon with the same number. They look in the hole and there's an identical Srixon. One guy had an ace at the most famous par 3 in golf, but they don't know which one. Man, that's cruel."

And that's coming from a man who knows the meaning of the word cruel.

⌣ ●

Pebble Beach Golf Links, Pebble Beach, California, 1919

Nowhere makes a bigger deal of a hole in one than Pebble Beach, the place where simply scoring one is sufficient a memory to last a lifetime. But if you have the good fortune to ace at Pebble Beach, the clubhouse personnel will respond with a joy that will lead you to believe you did it all for them.

For that selfless reaction, thanks goes to head pro Chuck Dunbar. He's a generous man with a warm ready laugh, the kind of guy golfers are glad to see in a dream job you know he appreciates.

It's because of Dunbar that every ace gets written down in a leather-bound book and that every golfer gets a Pebble Beach congratulatory flag with the important details embroidered on the fabric. It's usually waiting for you by the time you float off the eighteenth green, on-course marshals having already radioed in the relevant numbers.

"We do it because we know that getting an ace, any ace, is a thrill of a lifetime for most golfers," Dunbar says. "Getting one on Pebble Beach is something every golfer dreams of doing. Making it special is the least we can do."

You're probably thinking, "What a guy!"

It gets better. It can't happen often because of the volume of golfers, but once in a while he gets to be the genie in the bottle that makes wishes come true. Ask Joe Goddard.

He's a seventeen-year-old lad from a tiny English town called Waterlooville. He wrote an unfailingly polite and charming letter to Dunbar saying that he and his father were coming to America to see California and that, please, sir, would it be all right if after everyone's done golfing, we could perhaps walk about the course and see the par 3 seventh and the other ocean holes?

"It was such a nice letter from such an earnest kid there was no way I was going to say no. I wrote him back and said he and his father would be welcome to see the course," Dunbar says.

When Goddard and his father arrived, the three had a nice chat and the boy turned to walk the course in the still ripe afternoon sun, a video camera at the ready, Dunbar stopped him with a question.

"You guys bring your sticks?"

"Yes, sir."

"Go get 'em."

He waived the $350 green fees and just like that made a dream come true. But there are some things even out of his hands. Higher powers took care of them.

"Well, it was just one of the greatest things I can ever remember," Dunbar says. "I'm sitting here and one of the marshals radios back that we'd had an ace on number seven. He said it was the Goddard kid."

The father had it all on tape. When they got home to England the heartwarming story ran in the local papers and was picked up by the wire services across the country. Joe Goddard sent one of the clips from the Waterlooville *News* back to Dunbar with a note of thanks that could never express how truly thankful he really was. How could it?

But Dunbar'd already gotten all the satisfaction anyone could ever hope for when that radio crackled the unlikely news that he'd helped make a boy's dream come true.

"I was just happy that I'd been able to contribute to a memory that will last a lifetime," he says. "It's something I'll never forget."

Truly, there are special places in heaven for guys like Dunbar. There are special places on earth for them, too.

One of them is called Pebble Beach.

ACE PLACE
The Hole in One Bistro at Kilkea Castle Hotel & Golf Club in Kilkea, Castledermot, County Kildare, Ireland, features live lobster as the house specialty. It is prepared by world master chef George Smith. Dress is casual—no denims—and reservations are recommended.

Bombs Away! High-Altitude Aces

ALL SHOTS REQUIRE the golfer to gauge direction, course contour, and the ever-changing elements. Get an ace at one of the following holes and you'll be able to brag that the ball was in the air so long you had to calculate the deliberate speed of the Earth's rotation into your aim so the ball wouldn't miss the green. These are some of the most dramatic tee-to-green elevation changes on any American golf course.

Jeremy Golf & Country Club, Park City, Utah, Number Four, 196 yards, 120-foot vertical drop

The cart path down from the tee used to feature a descending series of signs that read: "Slow," "Slower," and, finally, "Even Slower. We Mean It." The signs were removed after someone realized anyone needing written warnings of the cart path peril would be too dumb to know how to read in the first place.

There have only been six aces since the course opened in 1981. Six! This is one hole where one particular type of eagle is an endangered species. Pro Mike Worsham was designated at one event to spend his entire day whacking ball after ball at the hole as foursomes came through.

"The wind just swirls so much that it's really hard to get zeroed in. I must have hit 80 to 100 shots before I could really get my bearings. Finally, late in the day, I got one about two feet away. Haven't come close since."

⌐ ▬

Stonehenge Golf Course, Fairfield Glade, Tennessee, Number Fourteen, 140 yards, 120-foot vertical drop

The Maxfli balata grins crazily up at Stacy Miller from inside the desk where it does its lopsided loops every time the Tennessee pro jerks the drawer handle. Miller, thirty-seven, grins right back.

No ball perhaps that's ever been so drop-dead perfectly struck has ever endured such dirty mistreatment.

The last time he'd clubbed it—August 10, 1995—he'd hit it square on the sweet spot with a 9 iron at the 140-yard fourteenth hole at Stonehenge Golf Course in Fairfield Glade, Tennessee. The picturesque hole features a panoramic view of the Cumberland Mountains and a 120-foot vertical drop.

"It's only a 9 iron and the ball really sails," said Miller, the head pro at nearby Bear Trace at Cumberland Mountain. "I hit it clean, right at the hole. I knew it was going to be close."

Close? It was a near bull's-eye, only Miller would have to wait for the ball to land. And wait . . . and wait . . .

"It's such a steep drop and it was hit so high, it just took forever to come down."

Miller knows the value of good golf etiquette and encourages players to treat the course with respect, but this one shot turned him into the sort of vandal clubs tend to ban.

"It finally hit about two inches before the cup, buried into the green and just destroyed the cup. A hole in one."

When he made the long march down the hill, he saw the destruction. The earth was gashed two inches before the hole. It's trajectory cratered it in right onto the very edge of the immersed steel cup. Inside was a handful of dirt and turf and a ball whose smiley face was matched only by Miller's.

What Miller did may not have been pretty, but it got the job done. The rules of golf contain no restrictions against subterranean access.

Sugarloaf Golf Club, Carrabassett, Maine, Number Eleven, 190 yards, 122-foot vertical drop

Breathtaking views from way up on Sugarloaf Mountain allow the golfer to spy moose, bear, deer, coyote, and fox. You're so high up you feel like an eagle. Of course, if you're too afraid to peek over the edge, all your buddies will call you chicken.

The Cliffs at Possum Kingdom Lake, Graford, Texas, Number Fifteen, 162 yards, 148-foot vertical drop

Retaining walls to the left of the green, 8,500-square-foot pond on the right, woods and water in back. The only way anyone's going to bail around this green is with a parachute.

Hunter Station Golf Course, Tionesta, Pennsylvania, Number Seven, 167 yards, 166-foot vertical drop

They haven't filmed a climactic James Bond vs. the villain scene here yet, but they will. Yeah, the hole's got a cart path, but you'd probably feel more secure getting to the green via more appropriate transportation: a fireman's pole.

The view is pristine enough to draw non-golfing tourists from Europe to make the huff 'n' puffin' hike up the mountain to enjoy a nine-mile vista down the Allegheny River and into the unspoiled Allegheny National Park.

"All you see is river and woods," said owner Terri Obenrader. "There isn't even the roof of a shed in sight. It's really spectacular."

The hole used to be a par 4 with the current green serving as a landing area, but too many bold golfers went for the blind green with hazardous results. The common sense decision led to a better, more spectacular hole, one in which every golfer gets to stroke a satellite brushing tee shot and hope the ball will come down somewhere around the distant green sometime before dark.

Arrowhead Golf Club, Littleton, Colorado, Number Thirteen, 174 yards, 200-foot vertical drop

The tee is nestled between what pointy-headed geologists call a "cathedral rock formation." Funny, because from way up here in the thin air most golfers don't have a prayer of hitting the green. Most tee shots are in the air so long the USGA ought to check the balls for the controversial new "helium cores."

Gatlinburg Golf Club, Gatlinburg, Tennessee, Number Twelve, 194 yards, 200-foot vertical drop

They call it "Sky-Hi," and it's a lowdown shame you can't stand here all day swatting balls at the microscopic green more than twenty skyscraper stories below. You feel more bombardier than golfer on this tee, only you've dumped all your 200-pounders and the only explosive you can drop on that tiny enemy bridge is a hand grenade. Time to consider surrender.

Pro Jeff Curtis says the drop is so severe many golfers talk to the ball like they're confused parents and it's a misbehaving teenager.

"They hit their shots," Curtis says, "and then they start yelling, 'Get up! No . . . get down!' The ball's in the air long enough for them to change their minds three or four times before it lands way off somewhere they didn't expect."

Waterfall Country Club, Lake Burton, Georgia, Number Two, 186 yards, 215-foot, gulp, vertical drop

Yeah, there's water, bunkers, and woods, but the most dangerous hazard here is crippling vertigo. A picture worth 1,000 words? Check out the Web site (www.waterfallcountryclub.com) and you'll see inflation's gotten hold of clichés. The picture can be summed up in one: wow. Hit this green and the guys in the Space Shuttle will see you smile.

Elfego Baca Golf Club, Socorro Peak, New Mexico, 2,414 yards, 2,500-foot vertical drop

Yeah, it's not really a course and, yeah, it's mostly a bunch of guys out to have fun on a mountain. Nothing serious—except that vertical drop.

LUCKY SIGNS
Some Germans try to increase their luck by walking around all day with dyed green eggs in their pockets.

"Just Doin' My Job"— Professional Aces

GOLF, BY ITS VERY NATURE, is a solitary game played in bucolic surroundings. It's an individual sport: You against an opponent; you against the course; you against your personal best. Only at the professional level with hundreds of thousands of dollars at stake does a six-foot birdie putt on the seventy-second hole become compelling on a grand scale. But let's face it, even that would draw yawns from a considerable section of the sporting public who finds more appeal in watching souped-up automobiles traveling 155.883 miles per hour and hypnotically making a left turn every seventeen seconds. But a televised hole in one is something that will draw the eyes and attention of race fans, chess fiends, football widows, and misshapen bowlers. It is the one instance in golf where fans and nonfans will turn to one another and say, "Hey! Did you see that! A hole in one! Now, how on earth did that happen?"

It may be just one stroke of 270 others over a four-day event, but, oh, what a stroke.

Tiger's Moon Shot

It's hard to pick the peak of Tiger-mania, the one instance where everyone was transformed into some mass hysteria with the realization that they were in the midst of greatness. Such hysteria is not uncommon at old-time religious tent revivals where witnesses, swept up in the passion, speak in strange tongues and experience involuntary spasms of rapture.

Maybe a religious experience explains what happened during the third round at the 1997 Phoenix Open at the TPC of Scottsdale. Or maybe a better explanation was all that beer.

Either way, it was there that Woods aced the 162-yard par 3 sixteenth hole in front of more than 15,000 spirit-swilling fans. The galleries, which are filled by 120,000 fans on the weekends, is considered the most boisterous, uncouth, inappropriate, and drunken of all the Tour stops. They heckle the golfers, they roar during backswings, and generally behave as if they are waiting for a cage match to break out on the putting green. Tiger's ace nearly caused a riot and many of the crowd acted like lunatics, stemming from the Latin word "luna," or "moon."

The ace caused fans to rain empty beer cups on the tee box as Woods walked away smiling and bowing in a Styrofoam shower, all of which was captured by network cameras. The hysteria continued as Woods triumphantly strolled down the fairway and to the cup to retrieve his ball.

But raining empty beer cups, applauding, and hollering were an insufficient form of celebrating for fifteen greenside inebriates. They spontaneously dropped their drawers, turned around, and mooned Tiger.

It's not to be condoned, certainly, but at least they didn't yell, "You da man!"

Hogan's Nightmare

Ben Hogan once told this dream about having the greatest round in the history of golf . . . and it made him furious.

"I had a dream one time that I was standing on the first tee and I hit my drive and it went right in the hole. A hole in one. Then I went to the second hole and the same thing happened. Another hole in one. Then another and another. Through seventeen holes I had a perfect score of seventeen. Then I remember coming up to the last tee and hitting another shot that sailed onto the eighteenth green, bounced twice, rolled right at the hole . . . and just lipped out. I remember waking up madder than hell."

A Game of Inches

The 1878 Open Championship in Britain may have belonged to someone other than eventual champion Jamie Anderson had it not been for his partner, Andy Stuart, who was serving as a marker for Anderson's solo round.

Stuart noticed that Anderson's ball was teed up outside the markers on the seventeenth hole, an infraction that if uncorrected would lead to a disqualification. Anderson quickly thanked him and reteed to a proper position several inches safely within the tee markers. He then struck the shot and watched it daintily roll into the hole in one.

Not only did Stuart save him from disqualification, his direction may well have have been the difference in the ball acing or missing.

Anderson won the championship by one stroke.

Lousy Putter . . .

Sam Snead made thirty-seven career aces and made at least one with every club in his bag, except the putter.

Here's How It's Done

Johnny Miller was hosting a corporate outing at the Binks Forest Golf Club, a club he designed in south Florida. As is usually the case, Miller was stationed at a 150-yard par 3 over water where he would meet 'n' greet each group, take a picture, offer swing tips, and give a friendly wager for small stakes in which Miller would hit and offer an autographed dollar bill to anyone who beat his shot.

During the day a very unhappy player came in complaining he was hitting every shot fat and that the short hole gave him the willies.

Miller, in the September 2002 issue of *Golf Digest,* said that he told the player to find his "brush spot" on the turf, the place where the club would just tickle the top of the turf, a surefire way to get the ball airborne.

Miller's instant tip didn't take and the player dribbled one into the drink. Frustrated, he turned to Miller and said, "Let's see you try it."

He handed Miller, a lifelong righty, his left-handed 5 iron.

Miller told the magazine: "I teed the ball, swung left-handed, and let it fly. The ball bored through the slight headwind with a mild draw, hit the green, released, and rolled into the hole.

"'Will that do?' I asked the fellow as the rest of the foursome roared. He just couldn't reply. His mouth just hung open in surprise."

Miller called it the luckiest of the twenty-two aces he's hit in his career.

Take That, You Crybabies!

Tour golfers probably admit to a mixture of sadness and professional relief at the June 15, 2000, passing of legendary golf course architect Robert Trent Jones, Sr. The architect of twenty-one U.S. Open Championship venues, Jones felt it his duty to keep courses tough, but fair.

"The shattering of par without a proper challenge is a fraud," he was known to say. "I make them play par."

He didn't just use choice words to defend his designs, he also employed his golf sticks for deft response.

When Jones redesigned the fourth hole at Baltusrol Golf Club's Lower Course in Springfield, New Jersey, for the 1954 United States Open, members complained that a 165-yard par 3 over a pond was unfair. Jones agreed to play a round with club pro Johnny Farrell and two members while other members watched and waited for Jones to stumble.

At the controversial hole, Jones pulled out a 4 iron and hit his very first shot onto the green and right into the hole.

He turned to the assembled naysayers and said with a straight face, "Gentlemen, the hole is fair. Eminently fair."

Jones was ninety-three at his passing and his thoughts were on golf right up to the end. After suffering a stroke, he awoke in a hospital bed to find his two sons, Robert Trent, Jr., and Rees, both prominent architects in their own right, standing with looks of loving concern on their faces.

"What are you doing here?" he asked.

"You had a setback," he was told. "You had a stroke."

"Do I have to count it?" he asked.

You Are Getting Very Sleepy, er, I Mean, Lucky . . .

Think being aceless doesn't bother some pros? Think again. It bothered European Tour star Jamie Spence so much that he began seeing a hypnotherapist in the hopes the ticktock doc could unlock some door in his mind that Spence was convinced was keeping him from getting an ace.

He was told all he needed to do to start getting aces was to "visualize the ball going into the hole."

Sounds easy enough. Well, maybe it was. It sure worked for Spence.

Three tournaments after his session, he knocked home his first hole in one. He got his second the week after that.

LUCKY SIGN
Lottery players in Hong Kong pay to get special license plates displaying their lucky numbers.

Amazing Arnie

The National Hole-In-One Association estimates that a golfer will make an ace once every 12,600 times he or she tees it up on a par 3. Anyone expecting to do any better than that had better plan on being really, really lucky.

Or Arnold Palmer.

Palmer has the distinction of being the only known professional player to achieve consecutive aces on the same hole a mere twenty-four hours after he'd celebrated the same remarkable feat.

It was on the 186-yard third hole at the TPC at Avenel in Potomac, Maryland, during the 1986 Chrysler Cup Pro-Am. He'd used a 5 iron and the shot was the twelfth ace of his storied career.

The next day Palmer says he showed up at the hole and was surprised to see a network camera crew setting up behind the tee of the scenic, slightly downhill hole with the meandering creek running short and to the right of the spacious green.

"I asked, 'What are you guys doing here?'" Palmer recalls.

They were there to film him getting a rare hole in one, one said.

"I said, 'Sorry, fellas, but you're a day late. That was yesterday.' They just smiled."

The green is deep enough to, depending on pin placement, warrant a two-club swing selection. But Palmer's no fool.

"Yeah, I took the same 5 iron, took my swing, and, wouldn't you know it, it went right in the hole. I turned to that camera crew, smiled, and said, 'Is that what you're after?'"

Palmer doesn't remember what he did on the third hole before an early morning crowd that was straining at the gallery ropes expecting to see the impossible possibly happen again.

"I do remember this much: I didn't get a hole in one," he says, his voice betraying a bit of disappointment.

Now, that's a competitor.

Six Pin Nicks

During the 1939 U.S. Open, Byron Nelson hit a pin six times out of seventy-two holes, none of them dropping for an ace or a regular eagle. The shots were struck with six different clubs—wedge, 9 iron, 6 iron, 4 iron, 1 iron, and driver. The lucklessness led to a tie and an eighteen-hole Monday playoff he won with a seventy that included a pin-clicking eagle on the par-4 fourth hole.

I Told Ya So

Two words his caddie kept saying to David Toms during a Nike Tour even in Mexico. They were: 6 iron.

Toms kept saying, no, it's a 5 iron.

"Six iron," the caddie insisted.

Toms said, "No, I want to hit the 5 iron."

The pro is usually going to win these arguments and Toms did. He hit the 5 iron on the fifteenth hole and used the stubborn caddie to increase his motivation. It worked. Toms put the ball in the cup.

Three holes later it was Toms's turn to use just two words. He turned to the caddie and said, "You're fired."

Big Heart, Empty Pockets

Kelly Robbins walked away with nothing but a big heart after her first ace at a hole at the 2001 Australian Open where anyone acing was handed a check for $212,000. During a particularly long delay at the par 3 eleventh hole, she impetuously turned to caddie Chuck Parisi and said if she aced the hole, she'd give him half.

She duly put her 7-iron shot into the cup for her first hole in one as a professional. Half of the total hole-in-one bonus goes automatically to the Breast Cancer Research Fund. But Robbins said she would also give away her share. She said charities in her hometown of Mt. Pleasant, Michigan, would get $53,000 and Parisi would get the other half.

Robbins said she and Parisi had talked about holing out from the tee as they stood waiting to play.

"I told him I was going to hit it in and that I'd split it with him," she said. "I guess you say that often but you never think you are going to do it."

Robbins finished the championship at 3-over 291 and would have taken away more than double the winner, who receives $60,000.

Watch Out! That First Step's a Doozy

He may not be able to leap tall buildings in a single bound, but supergolfer Tiger Woods was able to hit a drive from the rooftop of one skyscraper to the rooftop of another. After accepting a reported $1 million appearance fee to play in the 2000 Deutsche Bank SAP Open, Woods took part in a hole-in-one contest that had him and Colin Montgomery atop one skyscraper in downtown Hamburg, Germany, shooting for a special hole atop another building 135 yards away across a busy downtown street in the middle of a shopping district.

Each player got three shots. A hole in one was worth $25,000. Sadly neither player aced, but the stunt did fulfill one of Tiger's dreams, according to a press release issued prior to the competition.

"I have always dreamed of playing golf on the rooftops of a big city . . ." Tiger said.

Pick a Club, any Club

R. Johnson of North Berwick, England, is a name that should live in infamy in every caddie shack throughout the land. He aced the fourteenth hole at Muirfield during the Open Championship in 1906, but no one can ever reveal the specifics of the stroke. Johnson played with only one club throughout—an adjustable head club.

After a Start like This, the Day Can Only Get Worse

Rains at the 2000 U.S. Open delayed many rounds on Friday and pushed them into near-dawn early Saturday as the mists from the Pacific Ocean were still enveloping the seventh green at Pebble Beach, where Todd Fischer took aim from 106 yards out with a sand wedge.

It must have been a beautiful sight to the thirty-year-old veteran of the mini-tour grinds. The ball sailing up against that blue sky and descending down, down, down on that green surface and, ahhh! right into the hole.

Acing the picturesque seventh hole at Pebble Beach is a great way to start any day, especially during the U.S. Open. For Fischer, it couldn't get any better.

And it didn't.

He parred the coast-hugging eighth and ninth holes but took a double-bogie on ten. To make the cut, Fischer needed to hole an eight-foot putt on the eighteenth much later that day. The putt slid mercilessly to the left of the cup and Fischer's dream of playing the final two rounds at the U.S. Open were dashed, his ace long forgotten.

"I could snap every club in my bag," he told reporters. "That's how I feel right now. I guess I'll go back to my life now. Back to the mini-tours. I've got a little two-day event coming up. It's in a town called Wendover, right on the border between Utah and Nevada. I don't even think there's a stoplight there."

That's golf for you.

One minute you're acing one of the most famous holes in golf, the next you're bound for Wendover.

You Looking at Me?

Better have your hair in place, your zipper up, and the piece of spinach brushed from your front tooth before you ace. Paul Azinger says a hole in one makes people stare long after the ball's dropped into the hole.

In 2000, he used a 9 iron at the Players Championship to ace the 145-yard seventeenth at the Sawgrass Stadium Course's infamous island green.

"When I hit it, it lined up perfectly," Azinger said. "Some guy in the back screamed that it was right at it, and it was. It took a perfectly straight bounce and just kept rolling. I couldn't believe it when it disappeared."

He said the walk to the green was something he'd remember forever.

"You're a little self-conscious because you know everyone's looking at you. It was something to cherish, just a special moment you may never have again."

Reach Out and Touch 'Em

Jan Stephenson is one of the few American golfers to experience the intense adulation an ace brings in Japan, a country rich in tradition. To the Japanese, an ace is a mystical event, one that, like a good marriage, should be celebrated and commemorated.

She was playing an exhibition there in 1985 when blind luck struck.

"It was an uphill shot," she says, "and I could see the hole. I hit a good one and then all I see were the tops of the heads jumping up and down. The Japanese, back then at least, were very reserved and respectful. They would politely clap for a good shot, but there were no uproars like we're used to seeing in America. But I could tell by their reaction that it must have gone in the hole."

It did. Much was made of the native Australian golfer and her miraculous shot. After the exhibition, Stephenson asked to use a phone for "personal matters," she says.

"I was having a pretty rocky time with a boyfriend of mine, and I wanted to call him at home to try and straighten things out. But that sure didn't work. We argued on the phone for an hour and forty-five minutes. Anyway, I got to the podium and they gave me a check for four thousand dollars because I had scored an ace there. They were so happy and pleased for me. But not two minutes later another guy comes up and very apologetically gives me a bill for thirty-two hundred dollars. It was from the overseas phone call!"

She admits the phone call was a thoughtless mistake, one from which she didn't learn.

"Yeah, I made another mistake after that. I wound up marrying the guy."

Tough Crowd

Tom Weiskopf told *Sports Illustrated* in 1997 that he'd made sixteen aces in both practice and competitive rounds and, yeah, it was always a thrill. In fact, it was such a thrill that he was disappointed when the shot didn't thrill others.

He said he was playing a practice round at Scotland's Carnoustie in advance of the 1975 British Open. He hit a wind-dancing shot at number eight that remarkably rolled into the hole. Yet, none of the gallery seemed enthused.

"Didn't you see my ball go in?" he asked two elderly Scots

bracing themselves against the gusts near the back of the green.

"Aye, laddie," said one.

"And you didn't even clap?" Weiskopf asked.

"Boot, laddie," said the other. "It didn't coont now, did it?"

Now, That's Impressive

Like Weiskopf, Bob Taylor of Leicester, England, drew stifled yawns when he used a 1 iron to ace the 188-yard sixteenth at Hunstanton Links during a practice round at the Eastern Counties Foursome Championships. The next day, the first round, he aced the same hole but stiffening winds at his back caused him to use a 6 iron.

The day after, his playing partner jokingly offered him million-to-one odds against hitting another hole in one for a third consecutive day. Lucky for him, Taylor'd figured his luck had run out.

Wrong. He aced it to become the only golfer known to have aced the same hole three days in a row.

LUCKY SIGN
In India, players rely on magical necklaces made from rocks and pebbles, which are passed down from one generation to the next.

Major Toms

It was the kind of shot that people who weren't there will say they were because it was something everyone wants to say they were a part of. You can bet it was something David Toms will never forget.

It was his 5 wood at the brutally tough 243-yard fifteenth hole at the 2001 PGA Championship at the Atlanta Athletic Club. For Toms, it was the kind of golf shot and circumstances that kids dream of hitting and it was one of the greatest aces in PGA history.

"It was the coolest shot I've ever hit," said Toms of what was his sixth career ace, three of which came during competition. "It was just the way it happened—the Saturday in a major in the last group with everyone watching. And I hit a perfect shot. It's not like it bounced off a tree or rolled short of the green or anything like that. It was a pretty timely shot."

The ball had landed on the front of the green, bounced twice and disappeared from sight.

Toms did not. The ace catapulted him into a lead he would not relinquish. He would win the 83rd PGA Championship, secure a spot on the 2002 Ryder Cup team, and begin to build a reputation as one of the Tour's best golfers.

Out on a Limb

Paul Fusco says the strangest ace he's ever seen was struck by one of the best iron players in the game of golf, two-time Master's champion Vijay Singh. Fusco was Singh's caddie during the 2000 PGA championship at Valhalla.

"Oh, that's one I'll never forget," Fusco says. "He hits a 3 iron and it starts going right for the trees. Nothing but trouble. It hits the trees all right, but then bounces off a branch to around the back of the green and just rolls and rolls and rolls—it just about took forever—and kept rolling until it—plop!—drops right in the cup!"

Sure, the Tour pros demean some aces as mere luck and no one doubts the role luck played in Singh's trunk tickler.

"He didn't care how it happened," Fusco says. "He was looking at a 4, but got to write a 1 down on the scorecard. It was a huge break."

⌣ ●

Toeing the Line

The strangest ace Russ Craver's ever seen in his many years of caddieing was struck by Tom Purtzer at the 1989 Candian Open. The ball was struck by Purtzer, but it was what the ball struck that made the difference.

"It hit off a woman's foot in the gallery and bounced right in the hole," Craver says. "I never saw anything like it. It goes off her foot! Now, if she sees the ball coming and moves that foot, then he's having to scramble to make par. Instead, she doesn't see it, it smacks off her toe and goes right in. Very strange."

⌣ ●

Seeing-Eye Ball

Logistically, only one ace in golf majors was more remarkable, although less timely, than Toms's. It was struck by Dr. Gil Morgan, an optometrist by trade, at the 250-yard eighth hole at Oakmont Country Club during the 1978 PGA Championship.

The shot started with a clear, crisp "click" off the face of Morgan's wood and ended several seconds later with the ball striking the flag and vanishing. The shot was so stunning there was a moment when the packed gallery didn't know how to react. After a day of watching balls land in the traps and across the generous green, fans were unprepared to see a ball swish right before their eyes.

Not an Ace, but Not Believable Either

Billy Foster said the most amazing spectacle he's ever seen in golf was not an ace during regulation, but it was something better during a practice round. Foster was Darren Clarke's caddie during a practice round at Valderrama in 2000.

Practicing with Clarke, Tiger Woods holed a 110-yard eagle on the third hole. At the same hole, Woods asked his caddie to drop a ball into a greenside bunker to test that lie. He holed that shot, too. Still, unsatisfied that something might be missing he said, "Let's try that again," and had his caddie toss another ball into the bunker. He holed that, too.

A hat trick.

"I've never seen anything like that," Foster said.

Hoch as in Stroke

Scott Hoch is the active Tour player with the most aces—twenty-seven, something he can't explain. Who could?

He did it again at the seventeenth hole at Bethpage Black during the 2002 U.S. Open. When reporters asked how he did it, he gave a shrugging sort of answer that couldn't have been put any better by Einstein.

"I happen to get lucky more often than other people," he said simply.

No one knows. He's bounced 'em in off rocks in streams, rolled 'em in, and lasered a few in with the assistance of the pin.

In 1987, he aced and won a $118,000 Rolls Royce; he opted for the money, saying, "I have young kids and the grape juice might stain the leather seats. Plus, I don't think it would fit through the drive-thru at Wendy's."

In 1986, doctors thought a dark mass on Hoch's two and a half-year-old son Cameron's leg might be cancerous. It turned out to be a rare bone infection called kingella kingae. It responded to treatment and today Cameron is healthy.

But Hoch never forgot the treatment his son received at the Orlando Regional Medical Center, nor the faces of the parents and children who didn't receive such good news.

Two weeks after failing to make a two and a half-foot putt to win the 1989 Masters, Hoch proved his resilience and generosity by winning a nail-biter of a playoff against Robert Wrenn to win the Las Vegas Open. He then announced into the winner's microphone that he would donate $100,000 to the hospital where he and his wife, Sally, has spent so many agonizing evenings.

Hoch said it was the least he could do.

No one needs to remind him he's a lucky man.

An Ace-sist

Andrew Magee got the first hole in one at a par 4 in PGA Tour history at the 333-yard seventeenth hole at the TPC of Scottsdale during the first round of the 2001 Phoenix Open. The well-struck tee shot bounded onto the green and was heading away from the pin, but was redirected right in the hole after striking Tom Byrum's putter.

Rather than celebrate, Magee stood on the distant tee scratching his head.

"It looked like a hole in one and sounded like a hole in one, but I still wasn't sure it was one," he said.

It was a bona fide albatross. Under the rules of golf, any outside interference with a ball is simply the rub of the green.

"It was the first putt Tom [Byrum] made all day," joked Rusty Uresti, who was caddying for Byrum's playing partner Gary Nicklaus.

Oddly Enough

WHEN FOUR PROFESSIONAL GOLFERS all incredibly aced the same hole in less than four hours at the 1989 U.S. Open at Oak Hill Country Club in Rochester, New York, respectable newspapers from around the country rushed to eager mathematicians to get them to compute the odds of such a fantastic, unprecedented occurrence.

The highly respectable *Boston Globe* contacted math professors at the University of Rochester and Harvard University, and number crunchers from the National Hole In One Association of Dallas and *Golf Digest,* and asked the learned educators from these four highly respectable institutions to give them their findings.

Golf Digest was the most ho-hum about the event, saying that the odds were a stingy 1 in 332,000, and that, statistically, the event was not likely to happen again until the year 2179 (it's never too early to get your Open tickets).

The National Hole In One Association said the odds were 1 in 8.7 million.

The University of Rochester professor said it was 1 in 10 million.

The calculators at Harvard produced a number that was said to be in the quadrillions, a number many of us never even knew existed. To be specific, Harvard said the chances of it happening were 1 in 1,890,000,000,000,000, give or take a couple of billion.

The only conclusion one could draw from these wildly divergent, astronomical numbers is that you wouldn't want the guy from Harvard taking over scorecard duties the next time you're out for low score to massage your ego.

Of course, the numbers are all utterly meaningless. You can almost imagine both the university guys coming out and announcing some made-up number with a straight face and then returning to the faculty lounge to spread the joke and start a chalk eraser fight with the madcap gang from anthropology.

Still, each and every time some golfer enjoys an unusual stroke of ace luck, most newspapers reach for, say, *Golf Digest* odds and transcribe them next to the feat as if they were handed down by Moses. Truly, the numbers might as well be made up—and who's to say they are not? Most mathematically challenged Americans can't even comprehend a rather routine number like 1 million. Start tossing around odds like 1 in 67 million and most of us begin nodding like chickens in the rain.

But because this volume aims at comprehensiveness, the most common and often used ace numbers are now included, but not endorsed as factual. As readers have already seen, any study of golf or aces does not comply with arithmetical formulas or other universal laws of practical science.

The most recent posting of those various *Golf Digest* odds came in the magazine's March 2000 issue and is touted as being "From the *Golf Digest* labs: The odds on making a hole in one."

The article says:

"*Golf Digest* has been the source for acer odds since the 1950s. To update them for the twenty-first century, we gave the latest numbers for rounds played each year (528 million) and estimated aces (100,000) to Francis Scheid, Ph.D., retired chairman of the mathematics department at Boston University. 'It's simple arithmetic,' Scheid says of the following scenarios, which assumes four par 3s of varying lengths in an eighteen-hole round."

A player making an ace in a given round: 5,000 to 1

Acing a designated hole in a single round: 20,000 to 1

Acing the same hole more than once in 1,000 rounds: 1 in 200

Getting an ace in a 1,000-round career: 1 in 5

Getting an ace in a 5,000-round career: Almost a sure thing

Two players, same foursome, acing same hole: 17 million to 1

Two players in a field of 200 acing same hole in a single round: 5,000 to 1

Two aces in a single round, same player: 67 million to 1

Three aces in a single round, same player: 2 trillion to 1

Most people are eager to embrace odds because they feel like they give us something reasonable to grasp in an unreasonable world. Odds help us state with equal confidence that there is no way we're going to get struck by lightning because the odds are against it, but, sure, many of us will line up to play the Powerball lottery because, hey, someone's gotta hit. Right?

Calculated Risks

The Centers for Disease Control and Prevention and the Harvard Center for Risk Analysis calculate the following odds of dying anywhere in the United States in a given year from the following causes are:

Heart disease: 1 in 397
Motor vehicle accident: 1 in 6,745
Homicide: 1 in 15,440
Drowning: 1 in 64,031
Bicycle accident: 1 in 376,165
Lightning: 1 in 4,478,159
Anthrax: 1 in 56,424,800

Of course, those odds are generic and can be manipulated if, say, you don't ride a bike much. And it's understood that anyone who wants to increase their chances of dying by lightning strike can do so by living in Florida's Lightning Alley (roughly Interstate 4 from Tampa to Orlando) in the thunder months of June, July, and August and if that's the way you really want to go, you can further reduce the odds by walking around wearing a five-foot metal spike on top of your head.

> **LUCKY SIGN**
> *In Russia, lottery players sometimes follow an old folklore tradition that says people who pin money to tree trunks will be rewarded many times over with good fortune.*

Unawed by the Odds

Bill Goss has made a living calling himself "The Luckiest Un-lucky Man Alive," in which he gives inspirational talks about defying the odds of death. In an April 1999 article in *Maxim* magazine, titled "He Gave Death the Finger 21 Times," Goss, a forty-six-year-old retired U.S. Navy lieutenant commander, reveals a timeline of doom that might have killed lesser men nearly two dozen times over. In his relatively short time on earth, Goss has been shot at, wrecked, rocked, chomped, crashed, crushed, and ravaged by a cancer so deadly the docs advised him to start making arrangements with the quiet fellows who tuck you in for the big dirt nap. He's survived car crashes, plane wrecks, mine cave-ins and through it all has believed in his chances of surviving anything over what the experts say in the actuarial tables. He's a man so upbeat that in 1994 when doctors told him an amelanotic melanoma, a particularly deadly form of cancer, would kill him in six months, he said, "At least they didn't say three months!"

He says odds are farcical contrivances in life. Unfortunately, he doesn't golf so there's no telling how lucky the luckiest unlucky man alive would be when it comes to aces. It would make some fascinating anecdotal evidence.

"The odds are just a way of trying to establish some sort of order and in life you just can't do that," he says. He's convinced that a positive attitude blows away any odds and he believes if he ever takes up golf, and someday he might, he'll knock aces in with regularity.

"People can certainly make their own luck," he says. "Truly believing you can do something is a powerfully positive mind-set. It helps you relax and can motivate you. I'm convinced that many golfers don't get an ace because they believe it's next to impossible. They hear all these odds that say, 'Oh, it's so rare, it's a miracle it ever happens.' That can lead to a very negative mind-set and that can lead to all kinds of physiological pitfalls that lead to actual negative results."

Goss and his once-skeptical doctors attribute his positive attitude to putting one of the meanest cancers into an early grave. Nine years later the disease is in full remission and this positive thinker is in demand throughout the country as a motivational speaker.

Both are positively remarkable developments.

Odd Facts

- The winning numbers for the New York Lottery on September 11, 2002 were 9-1-1. According to *Newsday,* lottery officials reported that in the last 5,000 plays of their numbers lottery, 9-1-1 was the winning number five times.

- At around the year 1900, an English statistician named Karl Pearson literally flipped a coin 24,000 times resulting in 12,012 heads and 11,988 tails. His results were a mere 24 tosses off from being a statistically perfect fifty-fifty.

- In the year 2002, *Mother Jones* magazine reported that the odds of being killed by terrorists while overseas were 1 in 650,000, while the odds of being dealt a royal flush in the opening hand of a poker game were about the same, 1 in 649,739. The magazine also reported the following:

    If someone were to purchase fifty Lotto tickets each week, they would win a jackpot once every 5,000 years.

    If your car gets twenty-five miles per gallon, and each Lotto ticket purchased equals a gallon of gas in your car, it would take 730 round trips to the moon before anyone won the jackpot.

It is three times more likely for a person driving ten miles to purchase a Lotto ticket to be killed in car accident along the way than to win the jackpot.

- When it was pointed out to Frank O. Keener, president of the Kentucky Lottery, that an analysis by the Louisville *Courier-Journal* that the odds of being struck and not killed by lightning were 1 in 709,260, but the odds of winning the Kentucky Lottery were 1 in 5,245,786, Keener responded: "I can tell you one thing, I'd much rather win the lottery."

Keener is right, according to Lee Trevino, one man who's experienced both, and a man who's often described as "happy-go-lucky."

Trevino was playing under seemingly innocent skies at the 1975 Western Open when an angry e-mail from the heavens came roaring down on a nearby lake where he, Jerry Heard, and Bobby Nichols were playing on separate fairways. Some luck.

Although many compare the odds to illustrate something unusual, Trevino says there is no comparison.

"I've made a lot of holes in one and have only been struck by lightning once. Believe me, a hole in one feels a helluva lot better."

- For what it's worth, this unattributed mind doodle was found on the Internet.

"It is frequently stated in books and articles on probability that if a succession of monkeys were set before a typewriter with limitless paper, eventually the complete works of Shakespeare would be repeated by chance. If there are fifty keys on the typewriter, the probability of the monkey getting Shakespeare correct is raised to the power of the number of characters (letters and spaces) in Shakespeare plus the adjustments of the typewriter needed for capitals and punctuation. On this basis the chance of a monkey typing the word Hamlet correctly is one in 15,625,000,000, so to quote the probability of his typing the complete works involves a large number indeed."

- The following item was found on the Web site of noted mathematician Dr. John A. Palous. It seems made up, but is presented as fact. Judge for yourself:

    "Bulletin: An exhaustive Wall Street study has revealed that 62.381527 percent of all statistics are made up on the spot."

Odds 'n' Ends

In essence, every odd or probability you've seen about holes in one, lightning strikes, and typing monkeys is fraught with leveling assumptions. In aces, it's assumed you're no better than the worst golfer to ever tee it up; with lightning it's assumed you don't know enough to stay safely indoors during a violent storm; with typing monkeys it's assumed we're talking about some run-of-the mill primate and not some a superintelligent monkey from another planet . . . or one from Earth's own future.

The only truly reliable odds can be found at the cold-blooded hands of people who make the determinations based on bucks. People in the insurance industry don't toss money around in a carefree way or rely on fanciful numbers that sound like they were invented to round off a Dr. Seuss sort of rhyme.

Doug Burkert is the president of the Dallas-based "National Hole In One Association" company. They are the lead insurers for most of the hole-in-one extravaganzas in the world where golfers aim for an ace and the chance to win cars, trips, or a million dollars. For them, it's a business in which they want to make money. They set their prices based on the cold, hard figures and would never monkey around with numbers for whimsical reasons. Since 1981, the group has been awarding on average $2.5 million to $3 million in prizes each year.

Burkert is a former public accountant who loves being in a job that gives away money to happy people. He says, "Sometimes I see these crazy numbers quoted in the paper and wonder where they come up with them. They're just incredible. I always see the *Golf Digest* numbers quoted for two in one round as 1 in 67 million, and I just don't believe that. It's just too high. The formula we use is simply the length of the hole, the number of shots, and the quality of contestants taking those shots. Of course, everything really changes if the players are professionals, the course has five or six par 3s or reachable par 4s. I tell you, statistics can really drive you crazy."

At last, a perfectly sane conclusion about all the odds.

Burkert says, the probability of an amateur golfer making an ace on a 165-yard hole are 1 in 12,600.

The probability of two holes in one on consecutive days by one golfer are 1 in 5,700,000.

The probability of two holes in one in the same round by one golfer are 1 in 26,500,000.

The probability of two holes in one on the same hole on back-to-back rounds by two golfers are 1 in 39,700,000.

An eminently logical man, Burkert is happy to dismiss the numbers with a logical postscript.

"Really," he says, "maybe the best way to look at it is every time an average golfer stands on a par 3, his odds of getting an ace are 1 in 12,600. It doesn't matter if he's never had one or if he just had one. It's sort of like flipping a penny and it'll all even out in the end."

For example, Burkert remembers one afternoon at the Woodlands where he stood for three hours watching golfer after golfer mishit shot after shot at a pin where his company was giving away $25,000 for an ace.

"Then all of a sudden this group comes up and gets three close," Burkert says. "The next group comes up and gets two close. The day's winding down and one of the last groups comes up and a guy hits one that lands on the front edge of the green—and this was the strange thing about it—the ball didn't roll, it didn't bounce, it didn't hop. It just landed on the front of the green and sort of skidded right in the hole. We go up and look in the hole and there it was, a big hunk of mud on its side. But all day no one had even sniffed the hole and then all of a sudden people started getting close and one guy nails it. Go figure."

When it comes to aces and odds, you just never know.

In its December 2002 issue, *Golf* magazine compiled the following stats and did the math.

Total PGA Tour aces since 1970
Total 859
Rounds played 612,206
Odds per round 712 to 1
Odds per hole 2,850 to 1

Twice as Nice

IF NO ONE'S GOING TO BELIEVE you when you tell them you just had an ace, just think how it feels when you've just aced twice in the same round. Or in consecutive rounds. Or, gulp, consecutive holes.

You can't believe it yourself. Those who've done one or the other say the feeling's similar to catching lightning in a bottle—then gulping it down. Forget all the astronomical odds. Getting two aces in one round is just . . . really weird. After all, many golfers go their entire lives without ever seeing an ace. Many more go the distance without getting one. To get one while you're still adjusting to the adrenaline rush of getting another is a mental and physiological overdose. By all the odds of probability, getting consecutive aces in any form is something that just shouldn't happen.

But, confound it, it does. The National Hole In One Association says it gets a handful each year, rarely more than a dozen.

387 Yards, Two Aces

By any standards the long shot generic odds of acing two holes in one round are astronomical. But the longer the shots, well, the longer the shots.

That's what makes what Mike Graves did at the Golden Bear Club at Keene's Pointe, Florida, seem as likely as getting struck by lightning while standing in line to cash in the winning Powerball lottery ticket.

He aced the 183-yard seventh hole and then repeated the feat on the 174-yard sixteenth. The aces were only the fifth and third respectively at the two-year-old Windermere, Florida, club. They were the third and fourth for the forty-four-year-old Graves, a 2-handicapper, who shot 69.

"The first one," he says, "I managed to stay kind of calm. I didn't want to ace and wind up shooting 78."

But when the second one dropped, so did his reserve. He and playing partner John Viera launched into a display of public euphoria that would have had pious Puritans running for their pitchforks.

"Oh, man, there was so much hugging and jumping around we damn near fell down," he says.

Graves, when informed of the odds, had to think long and hard as to which long shot—par 3s or Powerballs—was more priceless.

"Although it'd be against the advice of my accountant, I'd honestly have to say I'd rather have the two aces because it's just so unique. But then again, that's the same guy who says I spend way too much time golfing in the first place, so what's he know?"

And, No, It Wasn't the Tequila

Mark Roff had been golfing eighteen years when he walked into the pro shop to get a sleeve of balls for the last day of the three-day 1998 Le Master & Daniels Golf Tournament near his home in Spokane, Washington. They didn't have his preferred brand, Titleist DTs so he thought he'd try some Titleist Distance 100s.

Couldn't hurt. He hadn't exactly been burning up the Indian Canyon course with the DTs. He'd shot 85–85 the first two days.

He doesn't know whether it was the balls or whether he'd been secretly selected for some experiment in which supernatural golfing abilities are bestowed on otherwise ordinary golfers. Either way, it was about to start raining aces on and around Roff, who today is a thirty-nine-year-old insurance broker.

"I started out that day with an eagle, birdie, par, hole in one," Roff says. "After four holes I'm 6-under par."

Seven holes later he aced the 115-yard par-3 eleventh.

Well, that did it. Word got around that there was a guy on the back nine that had two aces and was 5-under after eleven. A crowd began to build. So did the pressure.

"The very next hole I rolled my tee shot and took an eight," Roff says. "It was something for which I was totally unprepared. I had never been in that position before. It was just so much pressure. My arms felt like pipes. Stuff like that's just not supposed to happen to me."

He was in the middle of a complete meltdown when one of his playing partners offered him a nip from a flask.

"You know, to this day I can't remember whether I took some or not. I was just floating around in this blur. These guys I'm playing with knew I had to settle down. The one guy says, 'Here, take some of this. It's tequila. You don't want to have two aces in a round and come out shooting something in the eighties.' I think I took some, but I can't say for certain whether or not I did."

A certain forgetfulness is sometimes associated with the consumption of tequila, so it's a safe bet he took a chug. Either way, he did settle down and finished with a 74. Plus, he won $1,200 for getting two closest to the pins.

"The bar bill cost me $520. The place was packed and everyone just got ripped on me, most of them were guys I didn't even know."

He didn't care. He was happy to have had an ace, then another, and to have survived his most tumultuous round. The local news crews showed up and he even got a call from the David Letterman show, but nothing ever happened of it.

That was all most people ever heard of Roff's amazing day. The funny thing was, it didn't end there.

"The next week I'm going with a guy from our office and he aced the third hole at the Coeur d'Alene Resort. One month later, I'm with a client from Seattle and we're watching a guy in front of us on a par 3. He aces. Then our group gets up there and one of our guys aces. In about one month, I had two aces in one round and saw three others. To this day, I haven't had one or seen one since that storm of them. I just can't explain it."

Roff says his two aces are remarked upon each and every time he golfs, and he still thinks about it all the time.

"Just once I'd like to get in that position again, just because this time I think I'd know how to handle it better. But I don't know whether something like that will ever happen again. Not to me, at least."

A Streak of Insanity

Many golfers say it's hard to perform after scoring their second ace in one round. If that's true, then it's a wonder Tom Doty didn't spontaneously combust during a remarkable October 1971 round at a course near his Chicago home.

His score was as follows: number 4, 500 yards, double eagle 2; number 5, 360-yard dogleg, hole in one; number 6, 175-yard par 3, hole in one; number 7, 375 yard, eagle.

Thus, his score was 2-1-1-2 for a remarkable 10 under par for four holes. No records of what happened next can be found.

Perhaps he did spontaneously combust.

For at least four holes he certainly was on fire.

Nothing Two It

Dick Houseal is a retired U.S. Air Force weapons mechanic who golfs like he's on a mission. Rain, sleet, even snow, he's golfed in conditions that would ground some of the planes at Eglin Air Force base in Florida, where he was stationed when he started learning the game more than forty years ago.

He's had nine aces in his life and the two in October 1983 that earned him some national attention didn't strike him as anything special.

"For me, it really wasn't that much of a thrill," Houseal says.

Here's what happened. He and his buddies were playing their regular round at Cool Creek Golf Club near York, Pennsylvania. The fourteenth hole is a 145-yard par 3 with a big drop. Houseal used a 6 iron.

"I didn't even see it go in," he says. "My buddy, Ernie Casino, yells, 'Dick, that went in the hole!' We get to the next hole, a 165-yarder and I just got done telling the guys in front of me that I'd had a hole in one when it was my turn to hit. Well, this took one bounce and then that went in, too."

He finished with a 68 that day. It wasn't until later that he learned just how special what he'd done was.

"One of the reporters said there had only been fourteen in the world who'd had back-to-back aces. I guess it was sort of special."

And . . . Action!

Suzan Toft, seventy-two, was happy to oblige a local film crew that had come to get her to tell her story of the ace she recorded at her home course in England in 1997. With cameras rolling, she drew back her club and hit the ball fair and true. The ball landed within a few feet of the hole and rolled right into the cup—an exact re-creation of her hole in one.

Scoring Sorcery

Jeff Cosey was going to take some brand-new clubs back home to Crofton, Maryland, to remember his April 2002 visit to see his brother, Brad, in Myrtle Beach, South Carolina. But thanks to some par 3 magic, he'll have more than new sticks to spark his recollection. A golfer for twenty-two years, Cosey, a 14-handicapper, considers himself average, but not a "hole in one" golfer.

"I was getting some new clubs and was using my brother's 8 iron at the 163-yard twelfth hole at the Witch," Cosey says. "I hit it and the ball disappeared. My brother yelled, 'I think you put it in the hole . . . You did it!' That was the first day."

The Witch and the Wizard are a nifty pair of Richard Lee–owned sister courses and both owe their names to the practitioners of the black arts. Had it been a different day in America, some Puritans might have been running after Cosey brandishing pitchforks.

Because two days later he got his second ace at the Wizard's seventeenth hole, a 155-yard par 3, in a round that included a holed sand wedge for eagle on a par 4.

Cosey says he doesn't use good luck symbols, potions, or spells, but that he was tempted to keep using his brother's clubs.

The Long and the Short of Ace Pairs

Retired policeman Freddie Crockett of Roanoke, Virginia, had been golfing twenty-six years without an ace in July of 2000 when he got to appreciate the full measure of the feat in under thirty minutes. The first came on the 336-yard, par 4, second hole, where Crockett used a driver. Just two holes later, he pulled out a sand wedge to ace the 104-yard fourth hole.

"It's simply unbelievable," Crockett, fifty-seven, said. "It's just like you're numb. I had a couple of buddies call me the next day and call me a lying son-of-a-gun. Well, I had two people who I've never met who saw it all happen."

Beat the Pro . . . Barely

Bill Simmons had to really be on top of his game at the Milburn Golf & Country Club in Overland Park, Kansas, to win a beat the pro contest back in June 2000. He had to be so on top of his game, that he had to make sure his ball was beneath the designated pro's.

Bill Maynard was the new course superintendent and was asked to fill in at the 133-yard par 3 fifteenth hole. One of the assistants couldn't make it and the head pro thought it would be a good way for Maynard to meet the members and, he hoped, make a good impression.

Well, he made an impression, all right.

Simmons hit first.

"His ball bounced twice and went right in the hole," Maynard, who was thirty-eight at the time, says. "Everyone goes crazy. I jump up on his back and start riding him around like a donkey. We're all having a great time. People from the other tees come by to celebrate all the commotion. It was great."

And it was just getting started.

Maynard made some bold comments about tying Simmons, remarks that produced bursts of laughter from the dozen or so people who had gathered.

"The ball was in the air and I knew it was going to be close," Maynard says. "Boy, was it. It went right in and capped his."

Of course Simmons won the prize, a set of irons, because the assistant club pro Scott Ehnes judiciously ruled Simmons's ball "was closest to the hole, because it was in first."

But the two had a good laugh, and Maynard was warned by other members his thunder-stealing ways better not happen again.

"I had one guy tell me, 'Maynard, if you'd have done that to me, I'd have beat your ass.'"

God Save the Queen, That's Remarkable!

As with much of ace lore, there are no accurate records kept on the rarity of two aces in one round, but the flabbergasted reaction of a spokesman for the Worldwide Hole-in-One Society in England is an indicator of its place in golf history.

Paul Chana, twenty-five, got two aces in one round at the Huntercombe Golf Course near London in October 2002. Chana, a 4-handicapper, said: "I was stunned. I was shaking. I certainly felt like I'd won the lottery. It's unbelievable."

The local paper said the odds of Chana's feat were 13 million to one (*Golf Digest* says it's 67 million to one, but maybe the enormous discrepancy's the result of the Brits doing some metric math).

But the spokesman for the Hole-in-One Society said: "I've only heard of this happening once before."

Some Turkey Talk About Eagles

Golf is a family affair for Syracuse, Indiana, native Derek Smith and his family. He was golfing in July 2002 with his uncles, Dave, Tom, Gary, and Jerry at the highly regarded and challenging Wolf Run Golf Club in Indianapolis where Derek's an assistant pro when Smith aced the 134-yard sixth hole and followed it up with an ace at the 192-yard thirteenth.

The family outing was part of an annual event where some of the male family members get together for golf. Then at Christmas, they are asked to discuss the relevant and interesting aspects about the round before the entire family.

"I was kidding them and asked who was giving the speech this year. They all just laughed and said, 'Who do you think?' It will definitely be good conversation over Christmas dinner."

Cruel Aces

No one ever said golf was fair. In fact, the annals of golf are so rife with many instances where it seems patently unfair that it's a wonder the game isn't outlawed in an effort to preserve sanity, matrimony, and the general welfare. Every round is marred by a nagging thought, "If only I'd used a 7 iron instead of the 6, I would have broken 100."

In fact, nearly every golfer who's attained the mythic status of having broken 60 points out with some chagrin that they could have had, gee, a 58, if he or she hadn't misread that putt on twelve.

Golf is so unfair that some of those who've experienced the one perfect shot in the game are still sometimes flogged by misfortune. The ace should be perfect, sublime. It should not be tainted with misgivings or what-might-have-beens. In any other game, it would not.

But this is golf. It'll find the cruelest ways to break your heart.

Congratulations! You're Still Not Rich

Dennis Nokes had been golfing for thirty years when he recorded his first ace at the Olympia Hills Golf and Conference Center in Universal City, Texas. And it was a thriller, too.

"Oh, you should have seen it," says Nokes, fifty, of Converse, Texas. "The day was overcast and there were twenty-five mph gusts. I was playing with my wife and I knew I'd hit it good, but we lost it. I jokingly told her, 'Hey, maybe I had a hole in one.'"

The pair walked to the green and saw only one ball. It was his wife Kathleen's. Dennis started checking the traps while Kathleen, a more optimistic sort, checked the cup. Yep, there was a ball in there.

"She saw the ball in the cup and thought someone from the last group had left it behind. Then she saw it was mine. She said, 'Oh, honey, come over heeeere!' It was a hole in one."

Ah, how perfect. Great shot. Wife as a witness. And what a happy ending, right?

Not so fast.

"The ace was at five P.M. Earlier that day, they'd had a contest at that same hole and anyone who'd aced could have won a million dollars. The contest ended at three P.M."

Ouch.

Ace Recipe

Next time someone offers to buy you a drink for an ace to celebrate their good fortune say, "Hole in one, please." If they look confused tell them the following drink recipe from www.mixed-drink.com:

1¾ ounces Scotch
¾ ounce vermouth
¼ teaspoon lemon juice
1 dash orange bitters
Ice

Shake all the ingredients with ice and strain into a rocks glass.

Best of Two, Please?

Toby Warden was a fair-shooting 8-handicapper one summer day at what used to be the Pine Valley Golf Course and is now the Stonegate Course in Lubbock, Texas. He plunked down $5.00 for five balls at a million-dollar shootout at a 165-yard par 3.

"Twenty guys hit and only three guys hit the green," Warden says. "I was the last to hit. There was a big crowd behind the green. I hit my shot and made it—a hole in one! The only problem was this was just the qualifying round. It was good enough to get me into the contest, but not good enough to win it."

Many golfers swing differently if there's something on the line, especially if it's a million dollars. It gets in their head and, therefore, the money rarely gets in their pocket.

But Warden was cool. He hit another near-perfect shot during the competition. But near perfect isn't good enough. Warden's ball landed six agonizing inches short.

Still, he got the $1,000 consolation prize for closest to the pin and was handed a big oversized check in a ceremony that had Warden waiting for the other shoe to drop. The rules stipulated that all the golfers had to be eighteen years or older.

Warden was only seventeen, and that ceremony wasn't going to take so long that he'd safely turn eighteen in time. Nobody ever carded him.

To this day, Warden, twenty-four, wonders if he'd have been carded had his ball rolled that extra six inches and if they'd have given him the jackpot.

A "Bairdie"

Ev Hanlon had had his fill of holes in one by 1965 when he got his third at the Avon County Club in Avon, Connecticut. He was so upset at the traditional treatment stemming from his first two aces that he did something shocking the third time he knocked the ball in the hole. He plucked the ball from the cup, declared it an unplayable lie, dropped and took a stroke for an eventual par.

He said: "I don't want that money to go to drunks. I'd rather see it go to some kind of charity or perhaps a caddie scholarship."

The effect was the same as if he'd done what could be called "shooting a 'Bairdie.'" That can be named in honor of thirty-nine-year-old Chris Baird of Greensburg, Pennsylvania. Baird in 1992 was playing the 143-yard sixth hole at nearby Pleasant Valley Golf Course in Bullskin Township. He hit a roaring hook out-of-bounds and over the trees on the left.

Everyone else hit and it was time for Baird to re-tee.

"In that situation, I'm hitting again and I was already disgusted," Baird says. "You just want to hit and get away from the scene of the crime. I hit and started walking back to the cart. Didn't even bother looking."

But the second ball shifted the scene from crime to sublime. It went straight in.

"Everyone was saying, 'Great! You got an ace! You're buying the drinks!' I said that's not an ace, that's a three. You give me the ace, then I'll buy you the drinks. But they wouldn't do that so it's no ace in my book."

Amazingly, ten years later, the exact same thing happened on the exact same hole: another Bairdie.

"I couldn't believe it," Baird says. "Same thing happened, too. All the guys wanted me to buy them drinks again, but I said no. That's not an ace. It's a three. I had a penalty stroke. I still don't consider that I've ever had an ace."

But he's had something even rarer than an ace. He's had two "Bairdies."

Fred Couples has only one ace on Tour, but he did card a "Bairdie" at the famous island green, the seventeenth at Sawgrass, but "Bairdies" don't count. Ask Baird.

Hooky Ace I

Bobby Cheung had been a dedicated weekend golfer and a model employee at ABC7 News in Los Angeles when the temperate winds and the temptation of golf beckoned him to commit a venal sin familiar to most golfers. He lied to the boss.

Told him his back was acting up and he couldn't lug that big news camera all around the city in pursuit of fire trucks, police cruisers, and various news-making felons.

It was a tournament at Creek Course in Alison Viejo, California. It was a beautiful new course and the 1999 tournament included many of his colleagues from other area media outlets. Who was going to know?

In an ordinary round, no one.

But this was no ordinary round. Cheung, a 16-handicapper, aced the 143-yard sixth hole.

It was the first ace at the course and it was witnessed by more than eighty professional blabbermouths who get paid to report interesting and unusual feats. What Cheung did was, gulp, news.

"You don't understand," he pleaded. "This never happened. I wasn't even here!"

It was as if someone had taken compromising pictures of him with Jennifer Lopez. Your instinct is to brag about it, but you know the consequences would be painful if his wife found out.

His burden was lifted in 2000 when local columnist Wayne Freedman wrote about his plight and begged for mercy for Cheung saying, "He hit the luckiest shot of his life on the worst possible day and now he wants credit for it."

Cheung said, "I think the statute of limitations has passed."

$$\smile\ \bullet$$

Hooky Ace II

Johnny McPherson is a forty-seven-year-old middle school basketball coach in Austin, Texas. A father of two, Amy, three, and Grady, one, his life is filled with joyful squealings at home and then still more joyful squealings all day at work.

In fact, his ears are so often filled with joyful squealings there are times, he admits, when he wants to run out in traffic and scream. But that sort of release would be uncivilized.

Instead, he golfs.

He does so even at times when his most unruly students know he shouldn't. Of course, that's when maybe he needs to the most.

"I had all morning classes this one day," he says. "It was a beautiful day in January with temperatures in the eighties. I just had to make up an excuse and get out and play. So I skipped our of work early and didn't bother to tell my wife, who was home with the kids."

Only convicts on the lam could probably relate to the joyful sense of escape McPherson was enjoying. Then it got even better.

At the 120-yard eighth hole at Circle C Ranch in Austin, McPherson used a pitching wedge to ace, his first ever (he'd had a double eagle in 1996).

"I always say before I tee up on a par 3, 'Boy, this ball will look great in my trophy case back home.' I've always really wanted one, so this was great."

Then reality set in.

"The guys I was playing with were these big construction workers and my ball rolled in the hole the instant the girl in the beer cart pulled up. One guy bought six beers right on the spot."

He spent the rest of the round working on a story to explain to his wife why he was so unreasonably happy—and broke.

A Charitable Ace

The J. P. McCarthy Foundation in Detroit was sponsoring the second annual event it calls "The Richest Day in Golf" in 2001. The idea is that the foundation converts one of the ritzy area clubs—in 2001 it was the Indianawood Golf & Country Club in Lake Orion, Michigan—into an eighteen-hole par 3 course and signs up golfers and corporate sponsors who donate big bucks to play. Each and every golfer gets $1 million for each hole in one and a really lucky golfer could conceivably walk off the course $18 million richer.

Besides big money, the event draws big names. Rush Limbaugh was the celebrity in Michael Grimaldi's foursome when the General Motors sales vice president aced a $1 million hole in one. The only problem was General Motors paid Grimaldi's $5,000 entry fee and, yup, felt entitled to the loot. A compromise was reached when General Motors "allowed" Grimaldi to donate the entire sum to eight charities of his choosing.

What, no rebate for the guy who made the shot?

It might have been the most socialistic compromise ever associated with Limbaugh.

Now You See It, Now You Don't!

It wasn't a mirage. You could touch it. Kick its tires, honk its melodious horn, inhale its fine Corinthian leather interior. And that's what Rudy Manfredi and many other golfers did on May 27, 1997, at a charity tournament at Granite Bay Country Club near Sacramento.

It was a Mercedes C230 and, according to the sign at the 155-yard third, was free to anyone who fired an ace there. While the other golfers may have merely lusted after the $31,035 car, Manfredi won it. He aced the hole.

But when he went to pick up the car he was informed that the car had been parked at the wrong hole! It should have been at the fourteenth hole, which was designated for hole-in-one insurance. The car was delivered to former head pro Jim Leisenring with instructions: "This car needs to go on the water hole," which Leisenring, who knew a thing or two about his own course, took to mean number three.

That brought the shouting lawyers all running to the fray. The car dealer sued the club, the club sued the car dealer, and

Manfredi sued everybody, including the sponsor—and you can bet he worried about looking like a bad guy for this—the St. Francis Girls High School and the Roman Catholic Archdiocese of Sacramento.

Of course, he was right to do so and justice prevailed. Two years after his lucky shot brought him instant joy, the courts brought him a cash settlement.

His attorney, Matthew Eason said, "The greatest vindication to Rudy was the acknowledgment by everyone involved that he did get the hole in one."

Luck and Loneliness

Golf is a forthright game where the individual is responsible for his or her own score. You're trusted to give an honest answer when the scorekeeper asks, "What'd ya have back there?" But an ace, like precious metals or nuclear launch codes, is too valuable to be entrusted to one person.

The rules of golf stipulate that for an ace to count it must be witnessed by someone other than the golfer who made it, and it must come during a regulation round of golf.

Pity poor John Murphy. No one's accusing the guy of being dishonest. That would be unfair.

But go ahead, call him unlucky. How else do you describe what happened to Murphy at the Wil-Mar Golf Club in Raleigh, North Carolina, back in 1982? While playing a round by himself, he holed his tee shot at the 175-yard fifth hole. But because he was utterly alone, Murphy knew the unwitnessed ace was not official.

So he finished the round engulfed in a bittersweet melancholy and then went to the clubhouse to tell his friend Hank

Grady, the assistant greens superintendent, about his ace. A sympathetic soul, Grady agreed to ride out to the fifth with his friend so he could at least relive all the precious details of his glorious shot.

He even stood while Murphy teed up a ball to give an even more thorough depiction of the happy moment. The depiction went beyond realism and straight to replay.

Murphy put it right in the hole. Again!

But his joy was, once again, short-lived, when he realized this ace couldn't be official either. He had only played one hole and there wasn't enough daylight left to complete a full round.

The sun would shine no more on Murphy and his amazing day.

Ace-Sorted Wonders

No EXPLANATION HERE, except to say that every ace, past and present, witnessed by millions or witnessed by none, means something wondrous to someone. It's a remarkable event and every ace story deserves to be told, often again and again. These are just a few of them.

This chapter is dedicated to the memory of Ron Magnuson, whose lucky ace ball and the signed scorecard (82) from that day still sits with a congratulatory certificate in the rec room of the Park Ridge, New Jersey, home where he lived. His family knew that one lucky shot meant so much to him that it devoted two of the three paragraphs of a New York *Times* profile of Magnuson to the day this happy, loving father got a hole in one.

"It was the proudest moment of his golf life," his wife, Audrey, told the *Times*.

Magnuson was one of 3,030 people who died in the terrorist attacks against the United States on September 11, 2001. On that beautiful fall day, the kind when every golfer wishes he or she were out golfing, Magnuson died near his desk on the 101st floor World Trade Center's north tower, where he worked as a consultant for Cantor Fitzgerald.

It wouldn't be maudlin for golfers to take a few seconds to think of men and women like Magnuson the next time they are lucky enough to be out golfing.

A Yankee Doodle Dandy

Dr. Rupert Friday picks up the phone and instantly makes it clear he has no patience for fools or salesmen. He hears an unfamiliar voice say the word "golf" and thinks "Unwanted solicitor! Hang up! Hang up!"

"I don't have time to read any more magazines, thank you and good-bye!"

Click.

A second call manages to convey the message that it's not a sales pitch. The caller's heard that the ninety-year-old Pittsburgher is an accomplished golfer with fourteen aces, three of them coming on the Fourth of July.

"Why, yes, that's true. And, let me tell you, each of them was special, but the ones on the Fourth of July, those were great. I can't explain it, but it sure was a great way to celebrate Independence Day. A hole in one on the Fourth of July, well, there's nothing like it. To have fourteen and have three of them happen on the Fourth of July was the greatest."

His Day Will Come

Ron del Barrio, golf pro to the stars, won't reveal the name, only to say he's a well-known muckety-muck in the financial world.

"Oh, you've probably heard of the guy," del Barrio says. "He's accomplished so much in life and business that you think he'd be satisfied, but he's not. He wants an ace. He's more committed to getting an ace than anyone I've ever met."

Del Barrio has been to his office. Its polished windows offer a panoramic view of a splendid city. The walls are adorned with professional and educational achievements and awards from top institutions throughout the country. But the one plaque above all the others, the one way up on top of the paneled walls, is devoid of details.

It sits there waiting for his very first hole-in-one ball.

"Every single time he gets on a par 3, he pulls out a new ball and before he hits he looks at his watch. He wants to make sure he gets all the details right. He's convinced that someday he'll get an ace and he wants to be ready to let all the powerful colleagues and clients who visit his office know that he got an ace. It means that much to him. Maybe someday he'll get it."

Maybe he already has.

In the Nick of Time

It's probably a good thing for George W. Bush that Texas golf writer Art Stricklin isn't interested in politics. Unlike Maine-native Bush, Stricklin is Texas through and through. Spend even a day or two with Art and you'll be convinced he's the most popular man in the Lone Star State.

In fact, spend a day or two with Art and you'll be convinced that if he was your passenger and your car broke down in the barren plains of West Texas, the first car to drive by on the lonely road would stop and the driver would say, "Howdy, stranger. Need some help? Well . . . I'll be, hey, is that Art in there? Hey, Art! You coming by for dinner? I can have Marge kill another chicken for you and your buddy here."

The man knows everyone.

That's why it was surprising that Stricklin was almost golfing alone when he needed someone more than ever.

"For me, it was always in the back of my mind," Stricklin said in the press tent while covering the 2002 Valero Texas Open at La Cantera Resort & Spa in San Antonio. "I thought the law of averages would catch up with me and someday I'd get an ace, but I was always worried, what if it happened when no one else was around."

It almost happened in 1996. Stricklin was playing a round at the Desert Inn course in Las Vegas. All alone. It was late in the afternoon and he was thinking about an 8 iron at a 146-yard par 3 when a stranger road up.

"Hi, mind if I join you?"

Art's a naturally hospitable sort who would gladly welcome potty-mouthed Ozzy Osbourne to a Baptist prayer meeting, so of course a fellow golfer was welcome.

Next shot—bang!—Art hits a hole in one.

Pandemonium. Just then the drink cart shows up.

"I'm going crazy and tell the guy, 'Get what you want, man, I can't thank you enough!' He's like, 'Well, what did I do?' I'm trying to tell him he made it all happen. If it wasn't for him, my first and only ace wouldn't have counted. It was my lucky day."

Actually, it was the lonesome stranger's lucky day. The guy's from Lubbock, a fellow Texan. Now, every time Art shows up in Lubbock he feels obliged to take his good luck charm out to dinner.

"Man, that's the least I can do," Art says. "He's my witness."

A Valuable Lesson

Gary D'Amato, longtime golf writer for the Milwaukee *Journal Sentinel*, says the most haunting ace story he's ever heard had to do with two competitors at a local amateur tournament who were locked in a fierce match against each other.

They came to a hole that had a slightly elevated green that concealed the results of any well-struck shots.

"Both of them hit what looked like really good shots," D'Amato says. "Both right at the stick, but neither of them can see where the balls stopped."

They go to the green and find one ball about two feet from the cup. The other in the hole.

"The only problem was both of them were playing the exact same type of ball with the exact same number. They couldn't tell whose was whose and who had the ace and who had the birdie."

An official was summoned. The ruling?

"Because they couldn't identify the ball, both of them had to declare a lost ball and head back to the tee and hit again."

Tee Party (Pooper)

D'Amato has his own haunting experience regarding the ace. Like most thoughtful golfers, he gauges the wind, yardage, and other conditions while standing on a tee box. And like most thoughtful golfers, he doesn't give a lot of thought to the precise placement of the tee in the ground. A golfer will think "left side" or "right side" of the tee box, but not "an eighth of an inch forward," or "two thirds of an inch backward."

Maybe we should.

D'Amato tells the story of his closest ace. He hit a great shot and knew it was close, but just how close he didn't know until approaching the green.

"I saw the ball was just hanging on the lip. It couldn't have been any closer without falling in. So, so close. It was agonizing. I got down on my knees and just blew on it gently. It fell right in. I wonder now if I'd have put that tee just a hair closer if today I'd have my ace."

If Those Hands Could Heal

Jim Flick is one of the most respected and gifted teachers in all of golf. Top Tour pros turn to him when they need to cure themselves of a slice or a hook that's gnarling up their Sunday runs. But if word ever gets out about his lesson with *Golf* magazine publisher Mark Ford, the American Medical Association's going to investigate. Or maybe the Vatican.

After all, lots of sick people drag themselves to doctors to get healthy, but when it comes to a sick swing, no one's more feverish than an otherwise healthy hacker.

A hole in one is frequently described as miraculous. It's something Flick can't explain, but describes mysteriously as a "strange lining up of all the stars. You can't explain it. No one can." What Flick did with Ford sounds so simple, but if only it were. This mini-miracle happened at the 175-yard fourth hole at Boyd Highlands Golf Club near Scottsdale.

"Mark's a great competitor and has a really nice golf swing," Flick says. "But like a lot of golfers he has trouble with alignment and doesn't use enough club."

Now, pay attention: Flick says most of the hazards on a golf course are directly in front of the green and that most golfers are too egotisical to use the proper club for the corresponding distance. Your machismo shouldn't be threatened by grabbing a 7 iron when everyone else is hitting 9s. Hit the club that's right for you.

At Boyd Highland, the right club for Ford was not the 6—it was the 5. Ford switched.

Another problem is that 80 percent of all golfers tend to incorrectly aim right.

"Then in the middle of their swings they have to start a rescue mission to bail out, but doing that during the swing is not a good idea," Flick says. "It needs to be done before the swing. I really stress proper alignment."

With Ford, Flick physically lined him up—"this elbow needs to come here, bring this foot back like so, and turn that club face in just a tad . . . there. Now, swing!"

It must have been something to watch. The ball soared off Ford's 5 iron and into the blue sky like a laser-guided rocket right at the target.

Flick saw the ball sailing through the air and said out loud, "That could be a spectacularly well-struck shot . . ."

See, he's a prophet, too.

Seconds later the ball landed with spry bounce and rolled right into the cup.

Ford, a 26-handicapper, remembers standing there with a perfect follow-through posed for posterity like he'd been taken from the top of a golf trophy and placed on the tee just for the occasion.

"I'm seeing the ball land perfectly in the hole—the logical side of my brain is thinking—impossible!" Ford says. "It's still hard for me to believe, but I have a witness. Every person has a unique learning style. Jim miraculously deduced mine and was able to help me visualize the swing that made the shot possible. I'd had my first hole in one and it was all because of Jim Flick."

Flick, understandably, downplays the miraculous aspects of the remarkable ace. He doesn't promise those kinds of results.

"No, that's never happened before," he said, "and it probably won't happen again."

And that's probably for the best. After all, no one wants to spend their days and nights being followed around by hordes of desperate, middle-aged golfers hysterically shouting, "Touch me! Touch me! Please, Jim, touch me!"

The Rarest Bird

Because of the circumstances and the rarity of the shot itself, the most remarkable shot ever struck in tournament golf may have been struck by Bob Gregorski of Cato, Wisconsin.

He was playing the Dairyland Open, June 10, 2001, at the Lake Wisconsin Country Club in Prairie du Sac. It was a nip-and-tuck final with golfers hoping for a birdie on the 512-yard par 5 eighteenth hole to vault them up the leader board.

Gregorski did them all one, no, two better. He made a double eagle 2 on the final hole in the amateur division of the tournament. There is nothing more rare in all of golf than the double eagle. To card one to win a tournament is unheard of.

As the Milwaukee *Journal Sentinel* reported in its coverage of the feat, up until that time there had been only seventy double eagles made on the PGA Tour since 1970 when record keeping commenced. None of them were to win a tournament. On the LPGA, only eighteen had been made since 1971 and, again, none to win a tournament.

To win a tournament with a double eagle, the course would have to end on a par 5 or a reachable par 4.

Coming into the final hole of the one-day, 36-hole tournament, Gregorski was tied with Gary Menzel of Milwaukee. Menzel birdied the final hole, but still lost by two strokes.

Gregorski said, "I hit a good drive and had 237 yards to the hole. I hit a 5 wood, it took one bounce and then disappeared."

The most famous double eagle in golf history was Gene Sarazen's "Shot Heard 'Round the World" at the 1934 Masters on the par 5 fifteenth hole where Sarazen's 5 wood found the cup. But that shot didn't win the tournament for him. It only put him in a position to do so in an eventual playoff with Craig Wood.

It was Gregorski's first double eagle and helped him recover from blowing an earlier four-stroke lead two holes earlier in which he'd hit two balls out-of-bounds on the way to making an eight.

Take That, You Surly Bag Dragger!

Ron Riemer's quest is to get the "Ace Slam," a hole in one at each of one of the venues that has hosted golf's four major championships. It's a noble aspiration for the sixty-three-year-old equipment advertising director for *Golf* magazine, and he's halfway there, but the one he got on the 190-yard tenth hole on the West Course at Winged Foot, a U.S. Open venue, in September 1992 already assures his inclusion in noteworthy aces.

It was there that he struck a blow for anyone who's ever been mistreated by a rude caddie, and he did it by striking an in-your-face ace. He did it, too, during a pressure situation when the eyes of his peers were all over him.

"There was a group on number eleven looking down at our tee and I was all ready to hit," Riemer says. "Then from around the hedge comes this caddie carrying two bags. He's making all kinds of noise and I want to do well so I back away and give him the stink-eye look."

The look was so offensive to the caddie that he decided to retaliate. After Riemer had composed himself and re-addressed the ball, the caddie deliberately and gratuitously let both bags drop to the ground—*clank! clank!*—just as Reimer was preparing to hit. He backed away again in a fury.

Imagine it happening to you. There are more than a dozen players and caddies observing this *mano a mano* duel being played out with stink eyes and banged bags and they're all watching you. You know the caddie wants to you to strip an embarrassing beaver pelt out of the plush tee and humiliate yourself, but you don't know if he's going to belch, wheeze, coo or whatever. But you have to hit, and that's what Riemer did.

Right in the hole.

"The guy wouldn't even look at me."

But you can bet everyone else did.

The One-Armed Bandit

You couldn't count on two hands all the aces Larry Alford's had, and that's a numeric luxury fate robbed him of in August 1991 when he was one of the most promising young golfers in America. Just two months earlier, he'd been tied with Tiger Woods going into the final round at the Dinah Shores/Mission Hills Tournament in California. An automobile accident nearly cost him his life. Today, he figures he got off easy.

It only cost him his left arm below the elbow and, he thought, his future. But the man who lost an arm and a dream today doesn't consider himself a victim. He considers himself lucky.

And who's to dispute him?

Since the accident, he's had three aces in competitive golf, and twelve more during corporate outings, including two back-to-back with the same ball on the 151-yard fifth hole at Cypress Wood near Houston.

"Oh, that was really cool," says the twenty-nine-year-old resident of The Woodlands, Texas. "The first one was one bounce and right in the hole. I ran down and got it and came back for the next group, and the exact same thing happened. I mean, it literally hit in the same ball mark from the last lucky ace."

A scratch golfer before the accident, today he's back to a 3 handicap using a special golf prosthesis (The Halford Grip) and has shot a 68. He does more than 150 tournaments a year. When people say he has an advantage because he's standing on the same tee hitting the same club over and over he has an easy rejoinder: "Hey, I take 'em anyway I can get 'em," he says. "I'm just happy to get 'em. I tell them, "I'm only doing it with one arm and you can't do it with two."

The Ace Needs One More Ace

Dr. Clayton Kelly Gross was an ace long before ever picking up a golf club. He is a decorated World War II ace with six and one-half aerial victories in the European Theatre of Operations. At eighty-two years old, one of the few regrets to which he confesses is that he didn't begin golfing until he was fifty-two.

He was sixty-five years old when he got his first ace and has had three since.

For the U.S. Air Force to consider one of its pilots an "ace," the pilot needs to shoot down five enemy aircraft. Gross has had four aces on the golf course and is on a mission to get that fifth.

"Oh, boy, that's what I want," he says. "That would make me an ace in the air and one on the golf course."

He flew Mustangs and Thunderbolts during the war and snickers when he hears some pilots talk about their fear in combat.

"Ha! I don't know who those guys were," he says. "No one I ever flew with was ever scared. We had tremendous confidence in ourselves and our aircrafts. And it was justified in that we shot down 5.7 of their aircraft for every one of ours they shot down."

He flew 105 missions over 400 combat hours. His voice still stirs with jubilant emotion when he talks about the day he shot down a Messerschmidt 202 jet airfighter that flew 100 mph faster than the one to which he was strapped.

"I really thought at that moment I could take on the world," he says. "There was a whole pack of them off in the distance and I wanted to go pick 'em all off one by one."

He can't equate the thrill of an ace, but says he still plays three or four times a week and you'd like to be there when he gets his fifth ace. It'll be a sight to see.

"It'll be the only time you'll ever see an eighty-two-year-old man jump ten feet straight in the air," he says. "That'll be a real thrill. Of course, for me flying combat missions was the most thrilling thing I've ever done in my life. Golf's great, but there's nothing like watching an enemy aircraft that's been trying to kill you blow up in front of your eyes. You don't get a bigger thrill than that."

Cup-Crowders

WHILE NOT HAVING AN ACE is nothing to be ashamed of, having a surfeit of them is not without its burdens. If the first words out of anyone's mouth when you tell them you've had a hole in one are: "You're kidding me," what do you think they'll say when you tell them you've had thirty? Or forty? Or fifty?

Golf is frequently—and rightly so—referred to as a gentleman's game. The tee term "you have the honors" is not without relevance. The honors are earned when a golfer posts an honorable score and gives his partners an honest answer.

Maybe that kind of exemplary behavior leaves the game wide open to cheats, too. Every golfer's played a round or two with someone who's deft with the foot wedge or forgetful with a stroke or two.

The hole in one is so inexplicable that many golfers who've never had or seen one refuse to believe it's possible. Claiming a gaudy number can actually make people bitter. But only if they let it. Here are some of the ace hall-of-famers and their stories.

Art Wall

The ball wasn't in the air very long when Art Wall hit. Many times, it wasn't on the putting surface for long either. The all-time Tour hole-in-one leader with forty-six, Art Wall knew you couldn't get the ball in the hole if it was up in the air.

"He always said to get the ball on the green as fast as possible," says Terry Hurst, the head pro at the Country Club of Scranton in northwest Pennsylvania. "Where other guys would hit a sand wedge, Art would always punch a 9 iron and make it take one big skip and get it down on the ground and rolling. He'd read the greens and let the breaks do all the work. He was a master around the greens with the short game."

That fact is evident in that Wall still shares the record for the par 3 course at Augusta National. But his ace numbers overshadowed everything this 1959 Masters champion ever did in golf. He knew that other players suspected he'd gotten all his aces on a short hole near his home in Honesdale, Pennsylvania. Many pros will incorrectly say he got all his aces at a dainty hole at Pocono Manor.

"He was such an honest and gracious man, the kind who would never hurt a bird," Hurst says. "It hurt him. He'd get quiet if someone brought it up and he'd always shy away from the subject."

By any measure, forty-six honest aces is remarkable. But to say there is one magical hole, as many do, that fattened the highly regarded Wall's ace total, is factually incorrect.

His son, Greg Wall, is the head pro at Pocono Manor. It was the course his father played out of, but didn't play with much regularity.

"To this day, someone comes into the clubhouse and tells a buddy that the number-seven hole on the East course here is where Art Wall got all his aces," Greg says. "It just isn't true. He never aced it. But it's the kind of hole that people think someone could ace over and over. It's only seventy-seven yards straight down. We've had stories about people throwing it in here, but my dad never did get one here. He didn't play here much."

To see where Wall got his aces you need to play Honesdale Golf Club. It's a nine-holer with three par 3s and a reachable par 4. It was there that he got a jump on his total. But the documented aces he had on Tour would still leave him as the PGA Tour King of Aces.

"He wasn't the kind of man who ever talked about it," Greg says. "He didn't talk much about anything. But a fact's a fact. For him, it overshadowed everything else he'd ever done. It came up in interviews, he was always introduced as the Tour King of Aces. It really got to be too much for him."

For your information, aces weren't the only thing Wall drained. Most of the family ace luck died with him November 1, 2001. His fifty-one-year-old son's only had one.

Alabama Slammer

Like most golfers, Mike Hilyer is eager to ace a par 3. But unlike most golfers, he knows the euphoria of getting a hole in one. In fact, he's done it ten times.

All on regulation par 4s. All verified by independent, sober witnesses. All certified by golf's governing body, the USGA.

Unfortunately, Hilyer didn't see any of them. "Too far away," he says.

The feat is so outlandish, the six-foot-five, 255-pound basher from Daphne, Alabama, doesn't even bother informing the local papers when it happens anymore. He knows someone else always will and he'd rather avoid the wrath of the skeptics.

Hilyer, fifty, has aced straight holes in sunshine and dog-legs at dusk. None has been at the same course, much less the same hole.

During the 1999 Gulf Shores Shrimp Festival tournament, he aced the 313-yarder that had been designated as the tourney's long-drive competition.

"I just signed my name and put the little stick right in the cup. Won a putter."

Gareth Clary is the veteran golf reporter for the Mobile *Register* whose typing fingers have to convince his readers of the feat's authenticity even as his own head screams, "No way! Can't be!"

"You figure maybe someone could luck up and do one, but ten?" Clary says. "I mean, c'mon!"

When people ask Clary if someone's making a sucker out of him, he points to the May 2000 *Golf Journal* article about Hilyer headlined, "FOURman." Clary says if Hilyer's aces are good enough for *Golf Journal* and the USGA, the magazine's publisher, then, heck, it's good enough for him.

The article only hints at the history of the owner of what may be the most quiet legend in golf. Hilyer, a 1970 draft pick of the Los Angeles Dodgers, didn't pick up a golf club until he was thirty-three years old. He shot a 93 the first time out. Backward. He played two months as a left-hander before a local pro told him he might be better off as a righty.

He didn't get his first ace until 1994 at the 356-yard first hole at the Pines in Millbrook, Alabama. After that, they started coming in bunches. In August 1995, he got two in one week.

He's aced par 4s in tournaments where gas-guzzling luxuries awaited anyone lucky enough to ace a par 3 (none did). Feeling guilty, organizers from the Alabama Homebuilder's

Association decided to do something really constructive and got him a VCR.

Now, every time he stands on the tee box of a par 3, he's consumed with acing it. Just, for once, to see the ball drop.

"That's all I think about on par 3s. Every time."

13 Aces, Same Hole

Joe Lucius holds the record for most aces on one hole, thirteen at the fifteenth hole at Mohawk Golf Club in Tiffin, Ohio.

"I've been told that every time he's made an ace the pin was in the same position," says Larry Baldridge at Mohawk. The 138-yard hole features a plaque dedicated to Lucius's feat.

Next time you're out at the course—the back nine's a Donald Ross design—and the pin's in the back left, think lucky.

This Duke's the Queen

It's a good thing Donna Duke didn't take up the game until she was fifty-one. Had she started it an earlier age, she'd have been obtained by government investigators to determine if she's an actual earthling. Because the ace record this seventy-two-year-old former civil worker for a navy missile range near Point Mugu, California, is otherworldly.

In just twenty-one years, she's had fifty-three holes in one. The first one occurred shortly after she took up the game. It was at a women's tournament at nearby Ojai Valley Country Club. She told *Golf* magazine's James Dodson, "I don't know if I've ever been more thrilled by anything in my life."

It must have been addicting. That inaugural ace was followed by three aces on three consecutive days at three different courses near her Camarillo Springs, California, home.

The aces all came during tournament play and were witnessed by twenty-five different people.

A local television station once asked to film her trying to make a hole in one. She did while warming up, before the camera man had started rolling. When he finally got to work, she put one inches away.

Her shots are low ropes that fly straight at the target and roll, roll, roll.

She said, "I've decided it's the overspin that makes the ball go in the hole."

She understands there are skeptics but says her aces have never been disputed by any of her playing partners, most of whom were opponents in tournament play.

"I don't know why any of them would cause controversy," she says. "I've never used my notoriety to make a single penny. That would compromise my amateur status. I love playing the game too much for that. The thing is, whatever it is, is just luck and, frankly, its something that seems to happen from time to time when I'm playing well but least expect it."

Mancil Davis, PGA King of Aces with Fifty-one

When the time comes to plant wisecracking Mancil Davis in that last great unplayable lie from which there are no mulligans, he'll need a generously sized tombstone to include all the hole-in-one graveyard puns. It's not often stonecutters get to put a hole-in-one king in one of their very own holes.

He's the PGA King of Aces and holds the world professional record for holes in one. Since the age of eleven when Mancil began playing golf, he has aced fifty holes and he also holds the world's record for double eagles—a remarkable ten. He's the only man who earns a nice living based solely on his ability of standing on a par 3 and socking the ball into the hole. Often in conjunction with the National Hole-In-One Association, Davis, of The Woodlands, Texas, gets paid to tell hole-in-one stories—he's heard more than any man or woman alive—as players tee it up to win up to $1 million in ace contest money in shootout events.

"For me any day on the right side of the divot's a good day," Davis says. "But to be earning my living based on something that gives people one of the most joyful experiences of their lives is a blessing. To golfers, a hole in one is like a grand-child. It's something they treasure forever. Their eyes light up when they tell the stories about them."

If that's the case, then Davis's eyes shine like the sun. Here are just a few ace facts from the King of Aces:

- He's had 50 aces, the PGA world record.
- He's had 10 double eagles, a world record.
- The combined yardage of his aces is 8,519 yards, more than 4.5 miles.
- His aces range from 124 to 379 yards.
- In 1967, he had three aces in five days and made eight for the year.
- He made at least one hole in one per year between 1967 and 1987.

He had his first ace at the age of eleven and by the time he was twelve, he and his father, Bob, were whisked from their Odessa, Texas, home and flown to New York to appear on the CBS game show *I've Got a Secret*. His secret stumped the panel of Henry Morgan, Bill Cullen, Bess Myerson, and Betsy Palmer.

He played junior golf with Ben Crenshaw and Tom Kite and played on the PGA Tour briefly in 1975. He quit the Tour, he says, to become a club pro because his caddie "earned more than I did."

He didn't have the complete game it takes to succeed, but he does excel at one aspect of the game, the aspect that most thrills amateur golfers.

His secret?

"I aim right at the hole," he says. "If you ask one hundred golfers, ninety-nine of them probably say they're aiming at the green. Plus I have tremendous confidence that I'm going to make it. I've been tested by psychologists and they've said my brain waves reveal I'm much more positive on a tee holding a 6 or 7 iron than if I'm holding the same club on a fairway."

And he never, ever uses a tee on the par 3.

When the National Hole-In-One Association began sponsoring $1 million hole-in-one contests in the early 1980s, it needed a pitchman. It called Art Wall Jr., who said no thanks.

Then it called Davis.

Today he travels the world rapping about aces to amazed golfers from Battambang to Baltimore.

"No matter where I go, someone's always coming up to me and telling me about their ace. The great thing is it's something anyone at any stage of the game can enjoy. Not everyone's going to know what it's like to win the Masters or break 70. But one day I got a letter from a kid who was six years old telling me about his hole in one. The very next letter was from an eighty-year-old guy who'd been golfing sixty years and finally got one. For me, it's great to be dealing with so many different people over such a happy occasion."

It helps, you see, that the King of Aces is a Prince of a Guy.

Had to Be There to Believe It

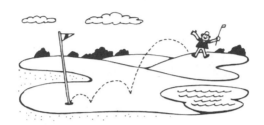

Luck, What Luck?

Who says PGA Tour pros don't care who drives first? Just ask Scott McCarron. It was August 2, 1999, at the CVS Charity Classic in Barrington, Rhode Island, when Lee Janzen pegged his ball and struck a sweet 8 iron on the par 3, 145-yard seventeenth hole. The hole had been designated for a special give-away by a local car dealer sponsoring the event. Janzen, McCarron, and Jim Furyk all celebrated Janzen's good fortune at carding the ace and winning the car.

Not so fast, McCarron said. He was sure that the Dodge Intrepid was meant for him.

Janzen thought he was kidding.

"You've got to get your ball out of the hole to make some room for mine," McCarron yelled to Janzen over the buzzing crowd.

"Yeah, right," Janzen thought.

Hitting right after Janzen, McCarron's shot headed directly for the flag. It bounced twice and spun right into the cup.

Incredibly, McCarron was the only one who wasn't surprised.

He told reporters, "After Lee's shot, I had a feeling I was going to make it. It was just one of those wild feelings."

Too bad for McCarron that he hadn't earned the honors. The car was awarded to the first player to ace the hole.

She's Not Horsin' Around

Jeanette Roberts used to ride horses on the rolling hills before Robert Trent Jones, Jr., began turning pleasant pastures into the modern classic that is the Granite Bay Golf Club. But when the course opened in 1994 her husband, Ken, bought her some clubs. After all, Jones said of the course outside Sacramento: "This course goes beyond golf architecture. It fits into that special category called art."

If that's the case, then Jeanette Roberts quickly made a case for being this superb gallery's curator. She understands Granite Bay's artistry, its structure, and, most of all, its par 3s.

A 36-handicapper at the time, she aced three of the courses par 3s in five rounds over eight days. She'd already had an ace just two years into her golfing career, but she was unprepared for the squall that came in March 12–20, 1998.

"They just kept going in," she says. "I couldn't believe it. I was thinking, 'Is this supposed to mean something in my life? Am I missing a clue?'"

Clues were about the only things she may have been missing. The first came on the slightly uphill par 3 third hole while she was by herself.

"Aha!" you're probably saying. "There were no witnesses! Doesn't count!"

Oh, there were witnesses—the most demanding and observant found anywhere on a golf course. There were three men on the green and she wanted to play through.

"Nobody wants to be held up on a golf course, but I was a single and these three guys decided to let me play through. I was so nervous! My goal was just to hit one shot, hope it made it to the green, pick up after one putt, and get out of there."

After the shot, no putter was necessary, and the three guys just got the heck out of her way.

Two days later Ken was walking off the eighteenth green and Jeanette was waiting for him after finishing the front nine. She said, "Stick around. I'm buying the drinks again. Got another one."

After she'd aced the par 3 seventh, the major news organizations began investigating. So did Eli Callaway and David Letterman; the latter flew her and Ken to New York, but couldn't think of anything to top her story. She got bumped. Callaway invited her down to Carlsbad, California, for a tour of the place where her lucky sticks were made.

As far as news coverage, friends in Singapore heard about it.

"One of our friends was traveling and was eager to read the sports pages in Singapore to find out about March Madness and the NCAA tournament. He said he was reading and there was a story about Granite Bay. He kept reading and saw it was me. He couldn't believe it."

Who could?

The news was so stunning the local newspapers resorted to math to try to grasp the solutions. They employed the chair of the Sacramento State math department to compute the odds of a 36-handicapper getting three aces in five rounds, which he claimed were 1 in 3 billion or about the same as zero coming up six straight times on the roulette wheel.

Jim Leisenring, the former head pro, took a more practical stand. He told her he was going to have to raise her hole-in-one insurance premium.

"He said I was becoming a liability."

Today, she's a 20-handicapper and hasn't had an ace since. Maybe her handicap's getting too low.

Cinderella Story

Once upon a time, there was a greenskeeper named Cary Sutinis at Hermitage Golf Course near Nashville.

If that name rings a bell then that's the only part of the story you know that's true. The rest is a legend that grows grander and more baroque each and every year. Too bad, too. The story's great enough that it doesn't need any fairy-tale embellishments.

First, here's the legend.

"These four guys were playing and they come to the eighteenth hole, a 320-yard par 4, a dogleg left with a big tree you have to clear to cut any of it off. Anyway, these guys are standing there and they see this grass-stained kid sitting there on a tractor. He's got a big chew in his mouth, shorts, and swamp boots up to his knees. Kid's never golfed before.

"Kid looks up at the guys and says, 'Mind if I try?' They all snicker, 'sure, kid, go ahead. It's the last hole. Give it a swipe.'"

"Kid stands up there and looks at the club for a few seconds before figuring out which end to hold. He tosses a ball on the ground—no tee. Then he takes a mighty swing and hits the ball. Ball clears the tree—and, I swear, you're not gonna believe it—ball goes right in the hole. A hole in one! Kid says, 'This game's too easy.' Hands the club back and walks away. Never golfed again."

That's the story. Here's the truth.

Sutinis, thirty-six, was indeed a greenskeeper's assistant at Hermitage in 1998, and he was riding around that day on his

EZ-Go maintenance tractor. He was dressed like a man ready to spend a day working cutting the grass and caring for the course—no one would have confused him with a paying customer.

"It was early and these four fun members come along and I decide to tag along for the back nine. I had time and I love to golf," says Sutinis, a 4-handicapper. "I didn't have my own bag, club, balls, or nothing. I was just tagging along and playing out of their bags. I'd grab a different club here and there."

On the eighteenth tee, he grabbed a driver and teed one up. Bang! He connected and sent a pill sailing clear over the obstructing tree. He'd reached the green here once or twice before but didn't hold any hopes that this shot was anything special. Boy, was he wrong.

"The guys on the green said it had rolled up right between 'em and dropped in like a putt. The flag was out. It one-hopped past the big bunker and rolled right up on the green and just dropped right in the hole. It was my first and only ace."

The story has all the elements of a legend and the one aspect that keeps earning the most embellishment is the boots, he says.

"Yeah, it always comes back to the boots. Every year the boots get bigger. They were work shoes, all right, but they weren't the big Carl Spackler from *Caddyshack* types. It was a thrill, but I was sorry I didn't get to see it drop. Right after that I went out and spent the next four to five hours watering greens."

All in a day's work.

Four Aces 1989 Open

It was hard to determine just who da man was one remark-able day at the 1989 U.S. Open at Oak Hill Country Club in Rochester, New York. It defies description. At the eighty-ninth playing of the venerable tournament, and though there had been thousands and thousands of rounds played, there had only been seventeen aces up until that June 16 day.

Yet on that early Friday morning, four players—Mark Wiebe, Doug Weaver, Jerry Pate, and Nick Price—in one hour, fifty minutes, aced the same hole, the 160-yard sixth hole aptly named Pinpoint. There are no records of such events, but it's likely that there were simultaneous marriage proposals among those in the stands and—who knows?—maybe even some children were conceived on the spot.

"You people certainly got your money's worth today!" roared Gary Player, one of the few non-acers, to the crowd that was roaring right back.

It started with the very first swing on the sixth that day by Doug Weaver. He hit a 7 iron, the club used by all four of the acers. Less than an hour later Mark Wiebe did the same thing.

Witness Jean Botsford of Ontario, New York, saw the whole thing. "I got to the hole a little before 8 A.M. . . . I'd say there weren't more than twenty-five people there. The first one was nice, Weaver's, but there was hardly anyone there to make much noise. Then, an hour later, came the next one, and by the time Pate came to the tee, there were thousands and thou-sands of people here. After the second one, I said, 'Well, to see two holes in one was fantastic.' After the third I didn't know what to say, but when the fourth came, I just blessed myself and said I now was part of history. It got to the point where we expected to see every shot go in."

When Pate's rolled in one voice was heard to sarcastically

yell above the din, "Big deal!" Right after that Price strode to the tee and dunked one.

Wiebe, the second of what became melodically known as the Four Aces, said, "My dad's played golf for thirty-five years and he's never had a hole in one. When I got to the tee, the guy there told me Weaver had gotten one. I said, 'That's great.' Then I took out my 7 iron . . . it goes in . . . the place goes absolutely bananas. The guy that told me about Weaver was doing cartwheels."

By then thousands of people had flocked to the hole to marvel at the hole.

Pate said he could tell his was going in as soon as he hit it.

"The first person I heard scream all the way to the hole was my wife. She's a screamer. Then up came Nicky. . ."

Price in the threesome behind Pate said the roar from Pate's ace frightened him. For the Englishman, the scares were just beginning.

"When that ball went in, it was the shock of my life," Price said. "I was in shock for about a minute. I've had three of them, but four of them on the same hole, the same day? I've played a lot of major championships and this is the strangest thing I've ever been a part of. If I hadn't been a part of it, I wouldn't have believed it."

Hubert Green came within four inches of acing after Price.

Outrageous odds were posted in newspapers around the country, but a professional bookmaker probably said it best. Tex Singletary, race book manager of Harrah's in Reno, a man who's seen his share of odds-defying long shots, told the *Boston Globe:* "I just don't believe it. Four holes in one? I can't believe it. The odds? They're astronomical. There is no such number for those sort of odds. It'd break the calculator trying to figure it out."

Right on the Money

The Real Lee Trevino

Lee Trevino's spent a lifetime disappointing strangers who come running every time they hear the name.

"They say, 'Where's Lee Trevino?' But they're always unhappy when they find out I am Lee Trevino."

This Lee Trevino was born Leora (Lee) Gilbert and didn't become Lee Trevino until 1973 when she married Eloy Trevino. Gender differences aside, the eighty-year-old grandmother and her famous namesake have something in common besides their monikers.

On November, 29, 1987, both remarkably got aces. She got hers, her first, with a 5 wood on the 119-yard thirteenth hole at Caloosa Golf and Country Club in Sun City Center, Florida.

"Oh, it was fantastic," she said.

Fantastic was probably a word that other fella used, too, but it's all a matter of perspective. He aced the seventeenth hole at the PGA West in La Quinta, California, during a Skins Game for a whopping $175,000.

Of course, that's peanuts compared to Trevino's ace at the 2001 ESPN Shootout at Treetops Resort in Gaylord, Michigan, where the rewards are somewhat extravagant. Trevino aced the 138-yard seventh to earn $1,010,000 ($1 million per ace, with $10,000 for being indisputably closest to the pin).

Oh, and in 1996, that other Lee Trevino aced again, too.

"I didn't even turn it in," she says. "The first one cost me a small fortune in clubhouse drinks and all I got out of it was a free bag tag."

Some days it just doesn't pay to be Lee Trevino.

. . . And the Other Guy

What are, perhaps, the two most famous aces of all time were struck by the same man. What are the odds? One was at one of the early Skins game extravaganzas in front of a huge television audience and won him $175,000. The other, which came fourteen years later, was the most lucrative single swing of a golf club in the history of the game.

What a lucky guy! Right?

Well, it's the same guy who nearly got killed when he got struck by a bolt of lightning in 1975. Did that make him an unlucky guy?

No, it makes him Lee Trevino.

"I've had six aces in competition, but none like those two at those exhibitions," Trevino says. "Those were unforgettable."

The Skins ace came at the zenith of the exhibition's popularity. Trevino was playing with Arnold Palmer, Fuzzy Zoeller, and Jack Nicklaus. Trevino remembers standing up at the tee looking at the flag on the 168-yard seventeenth at the PGA West at La Quinta.

"Not many people know this, but the Sunday round is taped," he says. "It was real early and the sun was just coming up over the horizon. I hit a fade 6 iron at the pin in the front right to this treacherous island green. We were all squinting into the sun."

The green location makes it hard for spectators to get around. That means there were just a handful of people near enough to verify the incredible.

"When the ball went in, none of us could tell. If you look at the tape you see us standing around, looking, and then we see the reaction of these five or six people behind the green. They go crazy. I tell Herman [Mitchell], my caddie, 'Hell, that ball went in the hole.' He jumps up and starts hugging me yelling, 'Thank you, Santa Claus! Thank you, Santa Claus!' To this day I don't know whether he was so excited he meant me or the guy from the North Pole."

Trevino made sure later that his longtime caddie had reason to thank him. In time, the IRS would step in and alter those thanks. Trevino earned $175,000 for that dramatic ace and $315,000 for the week. He gave Mitchell a generous share.

"Oh, that really opened up a can of worms for poor Herman. The IRS doesn't pay much attention when you're rolling along normal, but when they see a check in one week for twenty thousand or thirty thousand dollars, boy, that brought 'em running."

Just imagine their zeal when Trevino struck gold again in 2001. Trevino was playing with Paul Azinger, Phil Mickelson, and Raymond Floyd at the ESPN Par 3 Shootout at Rick Smith's Treetops Resort in Gaylord, Michigan, a place for which Trevino already had an affection.

"It is just a precious, precious place," he says. "The course is magnificent."

The format for the Par 3 Shootout can be called precious, too. Closest to the pin earns $10,000 and any hole in one gets

$1 million. Trevino nailed one at the seventh hole, a 140-yard shot with a steep drop. He hit a wedge clear back to the fringe behind the green that tilts sharply from back to front.

"The greens were soft so I knew I had to hit it long or it would spin right off the green. I hit it and thought it was long, I started hollering, 'Get down! Get down!' The ball hit and jumped back onto the green. Then it starts rolling. Raymond had just enough time to say, 'I think that ball's in the hole.' Then it dropped."

It was instantly the most lucrative single swing in the history of golf. Trevino got $1 million for the ace and $10,000 for being closest to the pin. Plus, there was $130,000 in Skins on the table. The format says that to win, you need to tie or beat everyone on the next hole. Trevino did that with a birdie, so with three swings he earned $1,130,000.

That's precious.

Organizers were thrilled because the ace drew international attention to the event. The thrill probably turned to fear when Mickelson nearly capped Trevino's ace. Remember, the tournament pays $1 million for each ace. Any cups that runneth over here will cause someone in the insurance industry to wince.

From the ace, Trevino got to keep $500,000 and donate $500,000 to his designated charity, the St. Jude Children's Research Hospital in Memphis.

Poor Herman didn't get a dime. He was in poor health and didn't carry his buddy's bag that week.

After what the IRS put him through in 1987, he may have felt an odd sense of relief.

The Million-Dollar Man

Jason Bohn didn't want to leave the house the day that changed his life. Not that he didn't want to get out of bed. At the time bed would have seemed like a hammock in a tropical paradise compared to where he was camping.

"I was asleep on the living room floor and my roommate had to drag me to my feet and beg me to go," Bohn says of that November 1 morning in 1992.

What could cause an otherwise able-bodied, promising young man to forgo the comfort of his bed to opt for the rigors of an element that would make a greedy chiropractor chuckle with glee.

Higher education. Yes, Bohn was a college boy, a walk-on sophomore golf scholarship recipient at the University of Alabama. He'd wound up there after deciding the obvious Northern universities near his Mifflinburg, Pennsylvania, home offered everything but temperatures conducive to year-round golf.

"And I always liked the Tide."

On this morning after a particularly raucous Halloween, the Crimson Tide could be glimpsed in his red, watery eyes. The last thing he felt like doing was participating in a hole-in-one contest to benefit the Jemison Society, a philanthropic group that was seeking to preserve a historic Tuscaloosa mansion that Bohn's Yankee ancestors had somehow failed to plunder.

It wasn't lingering Yankee spite that made him indifferent to the preservation of the old Jemison house. No, it was a hangover and a steadfast belief that he wasn't going to win. He'd never had an ace, a fact his childhood friend Brant Ficken was more than happy to relate.

"Yeah, Brant was my buddy from way back and he was

always telling me about his ace from when we were kids, always rubbing it in."

So with those grim circumstances, why not wait for the nausea to pass and for his head to return to its normal size? If he went, he'd still have the hangover, but attending the contest would silence the annoying yapping from at least one buddy. He'd get it over with and get home, this time to a bed.

He'd paid a buck for a ball and hit it within a 6-foot circle on a range to become one of 150 qualifiers. At the semifinals, each of the 150 would be given one opportunity to hit the stick and the ten closest would be taken to another hole with one shot at the ace. The Bohn name was called to go third.

"I remember thinking, 'Great! I'll swing and get the heck out of here. Go back to bed.'"

Really, he wasn't even trying. He just wanted to go home. But his shot was surprisingly true. It landed three feet, eight inches from the stick. He didn't eliminate himself. All he did was ensure that he'd spend the next three hours numbingly waiting for 147 other golfers to hit their shots in the humid Alabama sunshine.

"I hit that shot and just felt miserable. I just wanted to go home. Now, I was stuck there. I took a towel and went and lay down on a fairway. I was just dying."

By comparison, the living room floor was sounding like a Sealy Posturepedic. Finally, someone came to rouse him. Of course, he'd qualified for the finals. It was almost time to go home. The top ten—Bohn's was closest—were taken to a 135-yard par 3 at Harry Pritchard Golf Club and given a new ball. Contestants were not allowed to hit their own. Bohn was given a Top Flight number three and told he was hitting third.

Hmmm. Three and three. Seemed like a good omen.

Not that it mattered. What mattered was a bed, a couch, and maybe some Andy Griffith reruns on the TV. He wasn't thinking about his swing, course elements, or life-altering jackpots.

He tossed the Top Flight on the ground—no tee—he'd never done that before.

Two bounces and it went in.

Jason Bohn, nineteen, had won $1 million.

"I started sprinting down the fairway," he says. "I made it about fifty yards and nearly collapsed. My mind was saying, 'You've won a million dollars!' But my body was saying, 'You're hung over! If you take one more step you're gonna die!'"

Of course, his mind was relating something else as well. If you accept this money you will lose your amateur status, your scholarship, and probably the great friends on the golf team who will be heading down a different path than you.

Oh, he took the money all right. Jim and Carol Bohn didn't raise no fool.

He would, in essence, turn professional. The money would bankroll him in his quest to earn his Tour card.

But first things first. His body was still screaming at him to lie down, but the brain of a newly minted millionaire has other things on its mind. The party that had given him the hangover would have nothing on the party that was about to erupt. He told all his friends to round up all the cash they could get their hands on (he would be cash poor for the last time until the banks opened). The nine guys pooled together $1,100 and headed to the Brass Monkey in Tuscaloosa, where none of the bars opened until midnight on Sundays. Yeah, Alabama has a twenty-one drinking age, but, man, Bohn was feeling bulletproof.

"I handed the guy all the cash and told him anyone who walks through that door is on me. Just tell me when it's gone."

The local news crews had told him the footage was going to be picked up on *SportsCenter* that night, and it was. The anchor announced "Nineteen-year-old Jason Bohn won a million dollars," and that brought the owner over to the table of recently outed underagers. He said, "Hey, I won't say anything if you don't!"

They partied till 7 A.M. Jason had been awake and wired for most of the past forty-eight hours. But, really, the party was just beginning. The shot is paying him $50,000 a year for twenty years, and he says he's yet to touch the principal. The security it provided allowed him to chase his life's dream. He got a part-time job as an assistant pro at Tuscaloosa Country Club, earned his business degree, and set out on the mini-Tours.

On September 16, 2001, he posted an awesome 13-under-par 58 at the 6,407-yard Huron Oaks Golf Club in Bright's Grove, Ontario, in the final round on his way to winning the Canadian Tour's Bayer Championships. The round included, gulp, a bogie.

Today, Bohn's twenty-nine and has been happily married to Tewana since 1998. With each day and sub-par round at Q-school, he is becoming more confident that he will soon earn his Tour card. Oh, and he's had two more aces since the jackpot forced him to turn pro. One that won him $1,200 and another for $5,000.

Sure, they don't compare to the $1 million he won when he was hung over and wishing he'd been anywhere else, but they've been enough to let him reach out and touch his old friend Brant Ficken, who got an ace so long ago and has only his happy memory to show for it.

Payback's a bitch.

Paydays are not.

It's Over

IN BASEBALL, the greatest hitters are judged by the number of times they make it safely to base over the number of times they get to bat. It's their batting average and the greatest hitter of all time is legendary Hall of Famer Ty Cobb. The Georgia Peach had a career .366 batting average.

By that measure, the greatest golfer of all time is Kay Lowe, a professional opera singer who teaches voice at the University of South Florida near Tampa. When it comes to golf, Lowe is the only golfer in the history of the game to be batting 1.000. Each and every time she's swung a club on a regulation golf course, the ball's gone in the hole.

She's swung once, aced, and has never played again.

"I was dating this guy and he wanted to take me golfing," she says. "I went to a range to hit a few balls just so I wouldn't embarrass myself."

When they went to play a round at the lovely Hounds Ears Golf Course in Boone, North Carolina, she demurely rode along until they came to the picturesque fifteenth hole, a 110-yard par 3 with a steep drop. He asked her if she'd like to hit one. The gentleman even teed it up for her.

"It was the flukiest thing," she says. "I just hit the ball, it went flying through the air, landed on the green, and rolled right in the cup. I turned around and said, 'Is that good?' He couldn't believe it. He was screaming, 'You're a natural! That's the greatest thing that's ever happened on a golf course! It's a miracle!'"

She got into the cart. Rode off and has never played again. The opera singer just has no interest in golf. The fat lady had sung.

Lowe, by the way, is not your stereotypical opera singer. She's a petite five-foot-seven, 127 pounds. In Lowe's case, it's not over until the thin lady swings.

She swung and it's over.

—33—

About the Author

CHRIS RODELL (www.chrisrodell.com) is among the most widely read freelance writers in the world and the only one who's had simultaneous articles appear in *People, Maxim, Golf, National Enquirer,* and the South China *Morning Post*. He's the only golf writer who lives on Arnold Palmer Drive, one half mile from Latrobe Country Club and the King himself. He doesn't know Palmer, but their dogs were once good friends.

Register your hole in one with the United States Golf Register, the organization dedicated to identifying, documenting, and preserving for official record holes in one made in the United States. Should you join the ranks of aces, fill in the following form and mail to:

United States Golf Register
712 Milam Street, Suite 100
Shreveport, LA 71101
Telephone: 318-222-9606
Fax: 318-222-0229

(All entries with asterisks are required.)

*First Name: _____

Middle Initial: _____

*Last Name: _____

*Address: _____

*City: _____

*State: _____

*ZIP Code: _____

*Home Phone *(U.S. Golf Register use only):* _____

*E-mail: _____

*Course: _____

*Address: _____

*City: _____

*State: _____

*Course Par Rating: _____

*Date of Hole in One: _____

*Hole Number: _____

*Yardage: _____

*Ball: _____

*Club: _____

*Model: _____

*Manufacturer: _____

*Witness 1: _____

Witness 2: _____

Witness 3: _____

Witness 4: _____

Would you care to receive future correspondence from the
U.S. Golf Register via e-mail? (circle one)   yes   no

Comments: _____
_____
_____
_____
_____

How did you hear about the U.S. Golf Register? *Hole in One!*
*The Complete Book of Fact, Legend, and Lore of Golf's Luckiest
Shot* by Chris Rodell (ISBN: 0-7407-3631-0).

Please name all golf associations you are currently affiliated
with. _____
_____

(If none please write in "none.")

Please provide us with the name of your local newspaper.

_____

For more information, visit the United States Golf Register
Web site at www.usgolfregister.org or www.usgr.us.